T0277166

STEVE THE BARTENDER'S

COCKTAIL GUIDE

STEVE THE BARTENDER'S

COCKTAIL
GUIDE

TOOLS · TECHNIQUES · RECIPES   STEVEN ROENNFELDT

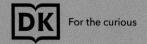

DK For the curious

Publisher Mike Sanders
Art & Design Director William Thomas
Senior Editor Ann Barton
Senior Designer Rebecca Batchelor
Proofreaders Lisa Himes, Lorraine Martindale
Indexer Beverlee Day

First American Edition, 2022
Published in the United States by DK Publishing
6081 E. 82nd Street, Indianapolis, IN 46250

22 23 24 25 26 10 9 8 7 6 5 4 3
003-328901-NOV2022

Published in the United States
by Dorling Kindersley Limited.

Library of Congress Catalog Number: 2022934279
ISBN: 978-0-7440-5871-0

DK books are available at special discounts when
purchased in bulk for sales promotions, premiums,
fundraising, or educational use. For details, contact:
SpecialSales@dk.com

Printed and bound in China

Cover photo by Meaghan Coles

For the curious
www.dk.com

MIX
Paper | Supporting
responsible forestry
FSC™ C018179

This book was made with Forest
Stewardship Council ™ certified
paper – one small step in DK's
commitment to a sustainable future.
**For more information go to
www.dk.com/our-green-pledge**

For my incredible wife, Kat.

*You support me with every project,
business venture, and idea that I have. This
book would not be possible without you.*

CONTENTS

APERITIVO

WHISKEY

GIN

INTRODUCTION

My YouTube journey started in 2015 when I uploaded a minute-and-a-half long video titled "Boston Shaker vs Cobbler Shaker." (Don't watch it; it's cringe-worthy!) I went all in and set myself an almost unachievable goal of uploading a cocktail video every day for an entire year, all whilst running a busy events business—appropriately named Steve the Bartender.

My channel has since grown into a community of well over half a million cocktail lovers, and my easy-to-follow cocktail videos have been viewed over 50 million times. I had no idea of the profound impact YouTube would have when I first started on the platform, but I find myself incredibly lucky and humbled to be surrounded by a community that is as passionate about drinks as I am.

Whilst I've had a career in bartending for twenty years and have been passionate about drinks for a long time, it wasn't until I started YouTube that I truly refined my craft. My channel simply documents what I've learned over these years through shaking, smiling, and thoroughly enjoying what I do.

One late evening in 2019, I consumed a few too many gin cocktails with close friends, and in our overly joyous state, we decided that we should open our own distillery. Within weeks we had a small-scale distillation set up, immediately started trialling gin recipes, and Threefold Distilling was born. Threefold shares the same philosophy I have for cocktails—classic combinations with a focus on flavour.

The goal of this cocktail guide is to share what I have learned and to help you understand the basics of cocktails. By the time you finish reading this book, my hope is that you discover a brief history of cocktails, understand cocktail classifications (also known as cocktail families), and have the ability and confidence to create your own unique cocktails.

The book begins with a brief history of mixed drinks and cocktail families before moving on to techniques. You'll find tips for making your own signature cocktails and creating easy menus when entertaining, as well as 125 classic and modern cocktail recipes.

Cheers!

A BRIEF HISTORY OF COCKTAILS

EARLY COCKTAILS

Cocktails are commonly thought of as an American innovation, but they are at least partly inspired by British punches—big bowls of spirits mixed with fruit and spices consumed in punch houses in the eighteenth century.
Fish House Punch (1732), page 268

Although the term "cocktail" is now used as a catch-all term for all mixed drinks, it hasn't always been this way. The first written definition of the word "cocktail" appeared in 1806 and described "a stimulating liquor composed of any kind of sugar, water, and bitters, vulgarly called a bittered sling." This combination of ingredients (with whiskey) is now referred to as the Old Fashioned.
Old Fashioned (1880), page 88

During the 1860s, it became increasingly common for ice to be harvested from lakes and transported to cities. Ice harvesting and the invention of an affordable ice machine meant that ice was more widely available, and mixed drinks flourished as a result. At this time, bartending was a highly respected profession.

In the second half of the 1800s, several highly influential bartender guides were published, including Jerry Thomas' *The Bartender's Guide* (1862) and Harry Johnson's *Bartender's Manual* (1888). These books shaped the bar industry and are still referenced to this day.
Manhattan (1882), page 80

THE PROHIBITION ERA

In 1920, Prohibition began in the United States, banning the manufacture, sale, and transportation of alcoholic beverages. Prohibition lasted for 13 years, but the temperance movement failed to achieve its goal of eliminating the consumption of liquor. However, the Prohibition era did fundamentally change social behaviours and drinking habits. Speakeasies were prolific, and for the first time, women sat alongside men in bars. Poor quality spirits such as "bathtub gin" were prevalent. Many of the great bartenders left America for more welcoming shores.
French 75 (1927), page 139

POST-PROHIBITION

In the years following the repeal of Prohibition in 1933, tiki bars flourished in the United States. Don the Beachcomber and Trader Vic led the way, creating classics such as the Zombie and the Mai Tai. These tiki-style drinks remained popular through the 1960s.
Mai Tai (1944), page 215

During the 1970s and 80s, craft cocktails declined in popularity and were replaced by vodka drinks, highballs, and disco cocktails.
Cosmopolitan (1980s), page 280

COCKTAIL RENAISSANCE

In the late 1990s, the cocktail scene started to shift, and long-forgotten pre-Prohibition cocktails were resurrected with fresh ingredients. Bartenders became celebrities again, much as they had been during the late 1800s.

The advancement of cocktails played out in a few key cities including New York, London, San Francisco, and Portland. Dale DeGroff, head bartender at the Rainbow Room in the 1990s, laid the foundation for the cocktail renaissance in New York, whilst Dick Bradsell was doing his part in London.

Sasha Petraske paved his way with the opening of the seminal New York cocktail bar Milk & Honey in 2000, whilst Audrey Saunders, Dale Degroff's protegé, went on to open one of New York's most iconic cocktail bars, Pegu Club, in 2005, which hosted the next generation of influential bartenders. These were just a few of the key players that kick-started modern cocktail culture.

This period of cocktail revival led to the creation of a multitude of modern classic cocktails such as the Fitzgerald (Dale DeGroff), the Dominicana (Sasha Petraske), the Earl Grey MarTEAni (Audrey Saunders), and the Penicillin (Sam Ross).

Today, bartenders are continuing to push the bar. Home bartenders are educating themselves and have a growing appreciation for the craft, whilst professional bartenders are creating new trends and redefining expectations. Sustainability is at the forefront of the drinks industry, and bartenders are pioneering new techniques to mix drinks by acid-modifying, fat-washing, distilling, clarifying, and more.

COCKTAIL TIMELINE

1783–1830
Punch is king.

1830–1885
The foundations of mixed drinks are laid.

Recipes are categorised into families.

Ice becomes commercially available.

1885–1920
Shaking becomes the popular technique.

Many of the classics are created during this era.

1920–1933
Era of Prohibition in the U.S.

Many cocktail bartenders leave the country.

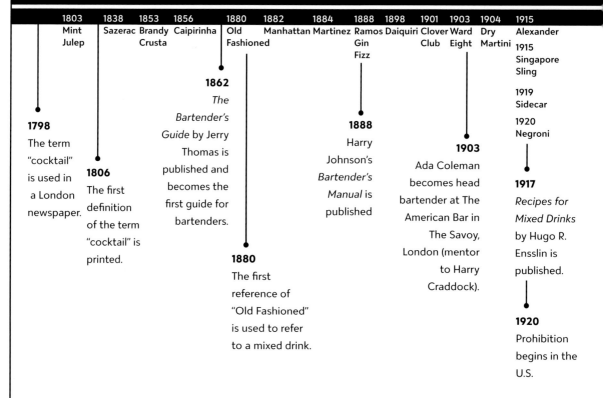

1800

1900

1920

1803	1838	1853	1856	1880	1882	1884	1888	1898	1901	1903	1904	1915
Mint Julep	Sazerac	Brandy Crusta	Caipirinha	Old Fashioned	Manhattan	Martinez	Ramos Gin Fizz	Daiquiri	Clover Club	Ward Eight	Dry Martini	Alexander

1798
The term "cocktail" is used in a London newspaper.

1806
The first definition of the term "cocktail" is printed.

1862
The Bartender's Guide by Jerry Thomas is published and becomes the first guide for bartenders.

1880
The first reference of "Old Fashioned" is used to refer to a mixed drink.

1888
Harry Johnson's *Bartender's Manual* is published

1903
Ada Coleman becomes head bartender at The American Bar in The Savoy, London (mentor to Harry Craddock).

1915
Singapore Sling

1919
Sidecar

1920
Negroni

1917
Recipes for Mixed Drinks by Hugo R. Ensslin is published.

1920
Prohibition begins in the U.S.

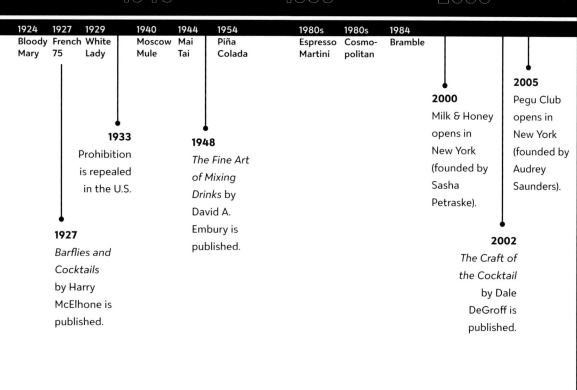

1920–1939
New cocktails
emerge from the
Caribbean and
Europe.

1945–1965
Tiki bars
become
popular.

The Martini is
famous.

Liqueurs are
popular flavour
modifiers.

1966–1990
Highballs and disco
drinks take over.

1991–2009
Technique-driven
cocktail bars emerge.

Premium ingredients are
readily available.

1940

1980

2000

1924	1927	1929		1940	1944	1954		1980s	1980s	1984
Bloody Mary	French 75	White Lady		Moscow Mule	Mai Tai	Piña Colada		Espresso Martini	Cosmo-politan	Bramble

1933
Prohibition
is repealed
in the U.S.

1948
*The Fine Art
of Mixing
Drinks* by
David A.
Embury is
published.

2000
Milk & Honey
opens in
New York
(founded by
Sasha
Petraske).

2005
Pegu Club
opens in
New York
(founded by
Audrey
Saunders).

1927
*Barflies and
Cocktails*
by Harry
McElhone is
published.

2002
*The Craft of
the Cocktail*
by Dale
DeGroff is
published.

COCKTAIL FAMILIES

Mixed drinks can be categorised into families according to their composition. This list of 12 modern categories will assist you in understanding the composition of various cocktails and their similarities and structures.

PUNCH (1632)

Punch is widely considered to be the earliest mixed drink from which all other mixed drinks have evolved. Traditionally it is prepared in advance, served as a communal affair, and consists of five ingredients: one part sour (lemon or lime juice), two parts sweet, three parts strong (arrack, rum, etc.), and four of weak (water, juice, tea, etc.), plus the addition of spice (nutmeg, cinnamon, etc.).

Fish House Punch, page 268

FLIP (LATE 1600s)

The term "flip" was first used to describe a mixture of beer, rum, and sugar heated with a red-hot iron. The drink evolved and was first referenced as a cold drink in 1874. A flip consists of spirit (or fortified wine), whole egg, and sweetener. Adding dairy creates a subcategory known as Nogs.

Sherry Flip, page 291

JULEP (1770)

The modern Julep consists of spirit (most commonly bourbon whiskey), water (through dilution), sugar, and mint. Early versions of the Julep didn't include bourbon or mint; they were simply a mix of rum, water, and sugar and were often made with cognac or French brandies. Peach brandy was also popular in New York in the 1830s.

Mint Julep, page 84

COCKTAIL (1806)

Although it is now used as a catch-all term for any type of mixed drink, "cocktail" was originally used to define a category of mixed drinks.

A cocktail was defined as a mixed drink consisting of spirit, water, sugar, and bitters.

Old Fashioned, page 88

COBBLER (1830s)

The Cobbler was by far the most popular mixed drink of the late 1800s. It consists of wine (or spirit), sugar, ice, and fruit.

Sherry is typically the most common choice of base ingredient.

Sherry Cobbler, page 292

SMASH (1830s)

The Smash family is a subcategory of Julep. The only difference between the two is the inclusion of seasonal fruit. Some historic recipes use seasonal fruit within the drink itself, whilst many simply use the fruit as a garnish atop the drink. The modern interpretation of the Smash is a cross between Sour and Julep, containing spirit, muddled fruit (citrus), herb (most commonly mint), sugar, and ice.

Whiskey Smash, page 112

SOUR (1856)

The Sour family of mixed drinks is one of the most popular styles of drink today. It's a single-serve descendant of the Punch, shaken and often served "up" (without ice). Drinks from this category have remained favourites, such as the Whiskey Sour, which was prominent from 1860 to 1960 and is still a mainstay on cocktail menus. The modern Sour format consists of 2 ounces (60ml) spirit, ¾ ounce (22.5ml) sweetener, and ¾ ounce (22.5ml) sour.

Whiskey Sour, page 115

COLLINS (1860s)

A Collins is essentially a sour cocktail that is lengthened with club soda and served over ice in a tall glass.

Tom Collins, page 175

VERMOUTH COCKTAILS (1869)

Gary Regan, author of *The Joy of Mixology*, categorised these as French-Italian drinks.

This category encapsulates any cocktail that contains sweet or dry vermouth, such as the Manhattan and Negroni.

Manhattan, page 80

FIZZ (1876)

The Fizz is a shorter version of the Collins served without ice.

Ramos Gin Fizz, page 164

HIGHBALL (1890s)

The Highball is the simplest category of cocktail consisting of only two ingredients—spirit and mixer. Mixed drinks such as the Moscow Mule, Cuba Libre, and Paloma fall into this category.

Gin & Tonic, page 143

TROPICAL (TIKI) (1930s)

Tiki "culture" emerged in the 1930s courtesy of Donn Beach (a.k.a. Don the Beachcomber). Tiki bars and restaurants thrived from the 1940s through the 1960s. Tiki drinks are known for their extravagant ingredient list, over-the-top garnishes, and South Pacific-inspired themes. Throughout the book, drinks in this category are referred to as "tropical" cocktails.

Mai Tai, page 215

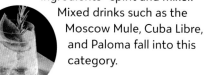

STOCKING YOUR BAR

Stocking your own bar is enjoyable and rewarding but it can quickly become a costly exercise. Pick a few favourite cocktails, purchase the select bottles needed, and expand your bottle collection gradually. (To start building your backbar, see pages 44–45 for cocktail menus that require minimal ingredients.)

TEN-BOTTLE BAR

If you want to go all out at once, these 10 bottles will enable you to make a long list of cocktails—many of which are featured in this book.

1. Whiskey (bourbon or rye)
2. Rum (lightly aged or aged)
3. London dry gin
4. Cognac
5. Blanco tequila
6. Cointreau
7. Campari
8. Sweet vermouth
9. Dry vermouth
10. Aromatic bitters

WHISKEY

The technique of distillation made its way from Europe to Scotland in the fifteenth century. Fermented grapes (wine) were commonly distilled in Europe but lack of availability led the Scots to use grain, which they had in abundance. They perfected the art of distillation and introduced it to America in the late eighteenth century. Famous names like Maker's Mark, George Dickel, and Jack Daniel's all have Scottish connections.

Whiskey is distilled from a fermented grain mash. A variety of grains (which may be malted) can be used in the mash bill, including barley, corn, rye, and wheat. The rules for production differ depending on the style of whiskey and the country in which it is made. Whiskey is typically produced in copper pot stills and aged in oak casks, although maturation time and the type of barrel can vary.

- **Bourbon whiskey** An American whiskey made from at least 51 percent corn and aged in a new, charred-oak barrel and produced in America. It has no minimum ageing period and needs to be bottled at 40 percent alcohol by volume (ABV) or higher. It is perceived as sweeter than other whiskies.

- **Rye whiskey** Made with at least 51 percent rye; other common ingredients include corn, barley, and wheat. In the U.S., rye whiskey also has to be aged in new, charred-oak barrels and bottled at a minimum of 40 percent ABV.

- **Scotch whisky** Must be produced in Scotland, aged for three or more years, and bottled at 40 percent ABV or higher. Malt whisky must use 100 percent malted barley and be distilled in a pot still. Grain whisky must be made with malted barley but can, and often does, include other cereals. Grain whisky is typically distilled in a continuous column still.

- **Islay whisky** There are nine active distilleries on the Scottish island of Islay. The island is largely composed of peat, which infuses smokey flavour during the kilning process of the malted barley, resulting in the island's signature peaty whiskies.

- **Irish whiskey** Often triple-distilled from unmalted barley that is blended with grain whiskey. It is typically referred to as being a smooth style of whiskey.

The word "whiskey" has two spellings. Scotland, Canada, and Japan prefer "whisky" whilst Australia, America, and Ireland prefer "whiskey." In this book, "whiskey" is used except when referring specifically to Scottish or Islay whisky.

RECOMMENDED BOTTLES

For whiskey cocktails, reach for a bourbon or rye whiskey, depending on your preference. Generally, bourbon will be a little sweeter whilst rye will be spicier. They are mostly interchangeable in cocktails, so you can start with one style of whiskey before expanding your backbar.

Bourbon	Rye	Scotch	Islay	Irish
Old Grand-Dad ($)	Old Overholt ($)	Dewars ($)	Laphroaig 10-yr ($$$$)	Tullamore DEW ($)
Four Roses ($)	Wild Turkey ($$)	Famous Grouse ($$)	Lagavulin 10-yr ($$$$)	Teeling Small Batch ($$$)
Wild Turkey 101 ($$)	Rittenhouse Bonded ($$)	Johnnie Walker Black ($$)	Ardbeg 10-yr ($$$$$)	Redbreast 12-yr ($$$$$)
Buffalo Trace ($$)		Monkey Shoulder ($$$)		
Elijah Craig Small Batch ($$)				

GIN

Gin is made by redistilling a high-proof neutral spirit. The high ABV (alcohol by volume) strips out most (but not all) of the flavour. The neutral spirit can be made from any starch or sugar base, such as wheat, grapes, potato, or molasses, each of which imparts its own subtle characteristics on the spirit.

The neutral spirit is distilled with an assortment of botanicals. To be called "gin" it must always include juniper and commonly includes other botanicals such as coriander seed, angelica root, orange peel, lemon peel, and orris root. The collected spirit is then diluted down to bottling strength with water.

- **London dry** A dry style of gin that highlights juniper and citrus. It's a versatile, classic style of gin that can stand up to bold ingredients. Despite the name, it doesn't have to be made in London.

- **Plymouth** A softer, earthy, citrusy and less juniper-forward style of gin that is distilled in Plymouth, England. An excellent choice of gin for mixed drinks and works well in more delicate cocktails with citrus or floral notes.

- **Old Tom** 150 years ago, Old Tom was the predominant gin available. It typically had a limited botanical bill, was made from grain, and was pot distilled, which results in a malty character. It was often sweetened or had a perceived sweetness from ingredients such as licorice root or fennel seed. Some Old Tom gins are also barrel aged.

- **Sloe** A gin-based liqueur popular in Britain, where sloe berries thrive. Fresh sloe berries are unpleasant and astringent but macerating in gin for months and sweetening results in a liqueur that is sweet and tart with notes of almond.

- **Contemporary** Many modern styles of gin highlight flavours other than juniper, such as citrus, spice, or savoury. Juniper must still be included in the list of botanicals.

Most of the recipes in this book don't call for a specific style of gin. In most cases, a classic London dry gin will work exceptionally well but experimentation with contemporary gins is encouraged. Thanks to the boom in craft spirits, there is an abundance of gins with their own unique botanicals that can be showcased in cocktails.

A classic London dry is the first bottle of gin you will need on your bar, as it is extremely versatile. Whilst there are differences between a London dry and Old Tom, you can comfortably substitute a London dry in place of Old Tom in a pinch.

LONDON DRY	PLYMOUTH	SLOE	OLD TOM	CONTEMPORARY
Beefeater ($)	Plymouth ($$$)	Haymans ($$)	Haymans ($$)	Threefold Aromatic ($$$$)
Tanqueray ($)		Plymouth ($$$)		
Fords ($$)				

RUM

Rum is made by distilling fermented sugar cane and its byproducts. The majority of distilleries make rum from molasses. The spirit can vary widely depending on the raw materials, fermentation, method of distillation, maturation, and blending.

Pot still rum is made in batches. Two distillations are required to produce a usable distillate of approximately 70 percent alcohol by volume (ABV). The spirit is full-bodied and full of flavour. Jamaican rums are great examples of full-flavoured rums that are predominantly made with pot stills.

A column still is more efficient for producing spirits and it can be run continuously rather than in batches. It requires less energy and yields are greater. Spirit produced by a column still can be distilled to a higher proof, which removes more impurities and results in a lighter style rum. Cuban and Puerto Rican rums are perfect examples of lighter-bodied rums that are produced using column stills.

It's common to blend the two types of distillates to create a medium-bodied rum.

- **Lightly aged** (1–4 years old) Colour may or may not be removed with charcoal filtering.

- **Aged** (5–14 years old) Definite influence of oak with notes of vanilla and wood.

- **Demerara** Originates from Guyana.

- **Black** Has little, if any, age with the addition of caramel and/or molasses.

- **Overproof** Describes a spirit over 57.15 percent ABV.

- **Spiced**   Has been flavoured with spices such as cinnamon, clove, nutmeg, allspice, vanilla, etc.

- **Rhum agricole** Made from fresh pressed sugarcane juice and typically exhibits grassy/vegetal notes.

- **Cachaça** A Brazilian spirit made from fresh pressed sugarcane juice that typically undergoes a single distillation.

RECOMMENDED BOTTLES

Most classic rum cocktails, such as the Daiquiri and the Mojito, use one style of rum. A lightly aged rum is a great place to start, but you'll likely want to pick up an aged rum (Jamaican, demerara, etc.) once you delve into the more complex, tiki-style drinks. Tropical (tiki) drinks often call for two to three rums for added depth of flavour.

LIGHTLY AGED	AGED	DEMERARA	OVERPROOF	RHUM AGRICOLE	CACHACA
Havana Club Blanco ($)	Appleton Estate Signature ($)	El Dorado 5-yr ($$)	Wray & Nephew ($$)	Clement Blanc ($$)	Leblon ($$)
Plantation 3 Stars ($)	Plantation Xaymaca ($$)	Hamilton 86 ($$)	Plantation OFTD ($$$)	Rhum JM Blanc ($$)	
Real McCoy 3-yr ($)	Denizen 8-yr ($$)		Smith & Cross ($$$)		
Banks 5 Island ($$$)	Appleton 8-yr ($$$)				

TEQUILA / MEZCAL

Tequila and mezcal are made from the core of the agave plant, also known as the "piña," but there are notable differences in the methods of production.

Tequila must be produced from blue agave (*agave tequilana weber*) and is typically steamed in industrial ovens before being distilled two to three times in copper pots. It is protected by AOC (controlled designation of origin) and can only be made in Jalisco, Guanajuato, Tamaulipas, Nayarit, or Michoacán.

Mezcal can be produced from any species of agave. Over 150 species of agave have been identified in Mexico, and the greatest diversity can be found in Oaxaca. Mezcal is traditionally roasted underground in pits lined with lava rocks before being distilled in clay pots. These methods of production give the spirit smokey characteristics, which are commonly associated with mezcal.

Mezcal is produced in nine areas in Mexico although 85 percent or more is made in Oaxaca. The most common variety of agave for mezcal production is espadín which accounts for up to 90 percent of mezcal.

Both tequila and mezcal are aged in oak barrels but categorisation is slightly different from one another.

AGEING	TEQUILA	MEZCAL
0–2 months	Blanco / Silver	Joven
2–12 months	Reposado	Reposado
1–3 years	Anejo	
1+ year		Anejo
3+ years	Extra Anejo	

RECOMMENDED BOTTLES

I recommend starting with a blanco tequila for mixing in cocktails. A blanco tequila is only aged for up to two months so it will exhibit fruity, peppery, and earthy agave notes, making it perfect for a **Margarita** (page 251) or **Paloma** (page 256). Adding a traditional mezcal to your backbar will bring more complex and smokey flavours to your drinks.

TEQUILA	MEZCAL
Olmeca Altos Plata ($$)	Del Maguey Vida Espadin ($$$)
El Tesoro Blanco ($$$$)	Banhez Artesanal Espadin & Barril ($$$$)

BRANDY / COGNAC

Brandy and cognac were extremely popular during the 1800s. The early bartender manuals by Jerry Thomas and Harry Johnson called for brandy in nearly a third of the recipes. In the late 1800s, an insect outbreak (phylloxera) wiped out much of the grape industry in France, limiting the availability of wine and brandy and encouraging the use of whiskey and other spirits in mixed drinks.

Brandy A distilled spirit produced from fermented fruit, grapes being the most common source. There are no origin restrictions, so it can be made anywhere in the world. However, there are regional styles, including cognac, pisco, and grappa, that may have their own rules and designations. Brandy is often aged in French or American oak barrels and unaged brandies are commonly referred to as *eau–de-vie*.

Cognac A grape brandy with a controlled designation of origin (AOC) with many rules to regulate its quality. The wine must be double-distilled in a Charentais copper pot still, bottled at a minimum of 40 percent ABV, and aged for a minimum of two years.

Age Statements

- VS—Very Special (2 years minimum ageing)

- VSOP—Very Superior Old Pale (4 years minimum ageing)

- XO—Extra Old (10 years minimum ageing*)

This was increased from 6 to 10 years in 2018

RECOMMENDED BOTTLES

Brandy has been made in France for over 500 years so it's safe to say that a French brandy or cognac (brandy made in the Cognac region in France) is a good place to start when stocking your backbar. You can opt for an inexpensive French brandy or upgrade to Pierre Ferrand 1840 Original Formula, which was crafted to recreate the style of cognac that would have been used in classic cocktails by nineteenth century bartenders.

- St-Remy VSOP French Brandy ($)

- Hennessy VS Cognac ($$$)

- Pierre Ferrand 1840 Cognac ($$$$)

VODKA

The first written reference to vodka came out of Poland in 1405 and by the 1500s, production was prominent in Poland, Russia, and Sweden. Unlike most other spirits, vodka can be made from countless base ingredients including wheat, potatoes, rye, barley, corn, and fruit.

Vodka is unaged and often referred to as an odourless and flavourless spirit, although this isn't entirely accurate. The flavour is far more subtle than other spirits and it varies based on fermentation, distillation, and the sugar or starch source. Wheat and barley may exhibit cereal notes, fruit-based vodka will be fruitier, and vodka from whey will be more textural.

Rules differ depending on the country but in the United States, vodka must be distilled to 95 percent ABV or higher.

RECOMMENDED BOTTLES

- Luksusowa ($)
- 42 Below ($)
- Tito's ($)
- Ketel One ($)

LIQUEURS

The origins of today's liqueurs are often attributed to thirteenth century monks and physicians who created herbal liqueurs for medicinal purposes. Liqueurs are classified as a distilled spirit sweetened with sugar and are often flavoured with fruit, herbs, and spices. This is an extremely broad category open to interpretation by producers.

RECOMMENDED BOTTLES

LIQUEUR	TASTING NOTES	RECOMMENDED
John D. Taylor's Velvet Falernum ($$)	Clove, lime, cinnamon, nutmeg	Saturn (page 167)
Mr Black Cold Brew Coffee Liqueur ($$)	Bittersweet, intense coffee, caramel, cacao	Dominicana (page 203)
Benedictine ($$$)	Citrus, nutmeg, sage	Vieux Carré (page 276)
Cointreau ($$$)	Sweet, fresh orange, floral	Sidecar (page 275)
Luxardo Apricot ($$$)	Apricot, almond, stone fruits	Charlie Chaplin (page 124)
Luxardo Maraschino ($$$)	Sweet, bitter cherry, nutty	Red Hook (page 96)
Pierre Ferrand Dry Curaçao ($$$)	Bitter orange, vanilla	Mai Tai (page 215)
St. Elizabeth Allspice Dram ($$$)	Cinnamon, nutmeg, clove	Three Dots and a Dash (page 239)
St-Germain Elderflower ($$$)	Sweet, citrus, lychee, floral	Irish Maid (page 76)
Suze Gentian Aperitif ($$$)	Earthy, bitter, floral	White Negroni (page 183)
Tempus Fugit Crème de Cacao ($$$)	Rich chocolate, vanilla bean	Brandy Alexander (page 260)
Green Chartreuse ($$$$)	Herbal, complex	Last Word (page 152)
Yellow Chartreuse ($$$$$$)	Honeyed, herbal, vanilla, saffron	Death Flip (page 248)

AMARO

Amaro, Italian for "bitter," is a bittersweet, herbal liqueur. Amaro is a broad category with a considerable variance between products. Typically a bitter liqueur is made using a base spirit that is flavoured with herbs, spices, and other botanicals and then sweetened. Many of the herbal ingredients are intended to aid digestion. Some amaro liqueurs are also aged in oak.

RECOMMENDED BOTTLES

AMARO	TASTING NOTES	RECOMMENDED
Amaro Averna ($$)	Cinnamon, cola, bitter orange, chocolate	Black Manhattan (page 59)
Aperol ($$)	Sweet, orange, grapefruit, rhubarb	Naked & Famous (page 252)
Campari ($$)	Strong bitterness, orange, grapefruit, quinine	Enzoni (page 136)
Cynar ($$)	Caramel, toffee, cinnamon, cola	Too Soon? (page 176)
Amaro Montenegro ($$$)	Sweet, subtle bitterness, bitter orange, cherry, floral notes	Cobble Hill (page 67)
Fernet Branca ($$$)	Intensely bitter, mint, saffron	Hanky Panky (page 148)
Amaro Nonino ($$$$$)	Vanilla, honey, orange	Paper Plane (page 92)

AROMATISED WINES

Aromatised wines are wines that have been fortified with the addition of alcohol and infused with aromatic botanicals. The majority are sweetened to varying degrees, which enhances the flavours. They are often bottled between 13 and 24 percent ABV.

Most aromatised wines have a white wine or mistelle base, and the colour is achieved through botanical maceration or by the addition of caramel. Mistelle is unfermented or slightly fermented grape juice fortified with alcohol. It is typically sweeter than wine because the sugars in the juice have not been metabolised by yeast.

A few subcategories of aromatised wines include vermouth, quinquina, and americano. They are defined by the use of, but not limited to, the following botanicals:

- Vermouth—wormwood

- Quinquina—cinchona bark (example: Lillet Blanc)

- Americano—gentian and wormwood (example: Cocchi Americano)

RECOMMENDED BOTTLES

DRY VERMOUTH	SWEET VERMOUTH	OTHER
Martini & Rossi Extra Dry ($)	Martini & Rossi Rosso ($)	Lillet Blanc ($)
Noilly Prat ($)	Cocchi Vermouth di Torino ($$)	Cocchi Americano ($$)
Dolin Dry ($)	Carpano Antica Formula ($$$)	Punt e Mes ($$)

Aromatised wines (and sherry) should be refrigerated to slow oxidisation. They are best consumed within a couple weeks but you can keep them fresher by using a wine pump.

SHERRY

Sherry is a fortified wine made from green grapes from the region of Jerez in Andalucia, Spain. Three towns make up what is known as the "sherry triangle" in Jerez. All sherry is made from Palomino, Moscatel, and Pedro Ximenez (PX) grapes, although Palomino accounts for 90 percent of all sherry.

Fino This type of sherry is aged under a layer of yeast, known as *flor*, that covers the wine and protects it from oxidisation in the barrel. Fino is fermented up to 13.5 percent ABV and fortified to 15 to 15.4 percent ABV, the ideal strength for a healthy flor. The barrel isn't completely full, which allows for this growth. As it ages, the barrel is topped up with new wine, providing food for the yeast. Finos are a more delicate style of sherry and the yeast imparts a nuttiness to the wine.

Manzanilla A fino sherry from Sanlucar de Barrameda. The town is located by the sea, which results in a lighter sherry with a hint of saline.

Amontillado This type of sherry starts off as a fino sherry under a growth of flor. Once the flor growth ceases, it is fortified to approximately 17 percent ABV and aged. Amontillados exhibit woodsy, fruit, and nut elements.

Oloroso Never aged under flor and fortified to approximately 17 percent ABV. This higher alcohol prohibits yeast growth. Oloroso is the darkest and most complex due to the longer ageing.

BITTERS

Bitters are typically made with a neutral spirit base that is infused with assorted botanicals such as herbs, spices, barks, and fruit. They have concentrated flavours and bitter notes and are intended for use in small amounts to flavour and season mixed drinks. There are a nearly endless variety of bitters available but these are the three essentials:

Aromatic bitters Angostura is the staple of aromatic bitters and should be the first on your bar. It exhibits notes of clove, cinnamon, gentian, and cinchona.

Orange bitters Many bartenders use a combination of Regans No. 6 Orange Bitters for its notes of cardamom, clove, and orange, and Fee Brothers West Indian Orange Bitters for its notes of sweet orange and cinnamon.

Peychaud's bitters Features notes of cherry, anise, and nutmeg and is an irreplaceable ingredient in both the **Sazerac** (page 107) and the **Vieux Carré** (page 276).

Other useful bitters:
- Xocolatl mole bitters—fantastic in a **Oaxaca Old Fashioned** (page 255).

- Chocolate bitters—try adding a chocolate accent to the **Negroni** (page 160).

- Celery bitters—add more savoury notes to a **Basil Smash** (page 119).

- Habanero bitters—spice up your **Margarita** (page 251).

- Lavender bitters—perfect for a floral take on the **Bees Knees** (page 120).

DIY SYRUPS + MIXERS

Sweeteners play a crucial role in cocktails by enhancing flavour and balancing acidity. Make small batches to keep your syrups fresh and always store them in the fridge. Don't forget to sterilise your bottles too!

SIMPLE SYRUP
(1:1 BY WEIGHT)

The most basic yet essential sweetener. Use superfine (caster sugar) which has small granules and can be easily dissolved with or without heat. Simple syrup has a 1:1 ratio of sugar to water by weight. Simple syrup is more forgiving when measuring than a rich syrup, which has a 2:1 ratio of sugar to water.

Keep refrigerated and use within 2 weeks.

Makes: 1⅔ cups

9 oz (250g) **superfine sugar**
9 oz (250g) **water**

1 Combine sugar and water.

2 Stir until the sugar is dissolved or shake it in a bottle.

RICH SYRUP
(2:1 BY WEIGHT)

Many people prefer to use rich syrup over simple syrup for its extended shelf life and lower water content, which results in a more viscous syrup. Rich syrup has 45 percent more sugar than simple syrup, so adjust recipes accordingly. Dividing the amount of simple syrup by 1.5 will result in the ideal volume of rich syrup. For example:

1 oz (30ml) ÷ 1.5 = ⅔ oz (20ml)

Keep refrigerated and use within 1 month.

Makes: 2½ cups

9 oz (250g) **water**
18 oz (500g) **superfine sugar**

1 In a saucepan, combine all ingredients and heat over medium-high heat until sugar is dissolved.

2 Remove from the heat and let cool before bottling.

DEMERARA SYRUP

Demerara sugar is a raw sugar extracted from sugarcane. It has had minimal processing resulting in more flavour and a golden-brown colour. Because of its richer flavour, demerara syrup is often called for in tropical drinks instead of simple syrup.

Keep refrigerated and use within 2 weeks.

Makes: 2½ cups

1 cup **water**
½ cup **demerara sugar**
1½ cups **superfine sugar**

1 In a saucepan, combine all ingredients and heat over medium-high heat until sugar is dissolved.

2 Remove from the heat and let cool before bottling.

HONEY SYRUP

Honey straight from the jar doesn't play nicely with ice. It hardens up and doesn't integrate into the drink, which is why it's best to make a syrup with the addition of a little water to thin out the honey.

Keep refrigerated and use within 1 month.

Makes: 1 ⅓ cups

1 cup **honey**

⅓ cup **hot water**

1 Combine the honey and water.

2 Stir until honey is dissolved and transfer to a bottle.

GINGER SYRUP

Whilst there aren't many drinks that call for ginger syrup, it is needed to make the modern classic Penicillin. In a pinch, you could use it in recipes that call for ginger liqueur given that most recipes would require only a small measurement.

Keep refrigerated and use within 2 weeks.

Makes: 1⅔ cups

1 cup fresh **ginger juice**

1¼ cups **superfine sugar**

1 Combine the ingredients.

2 Stir until sugar is dissolved and transfer to a bottle.

RASPBERRY SYRUP

Raspberry syrup is an essential ingredient to make a classic Clover Club. It's also a good base recipe to follow when making your own fruit flavoured syrups that can be used as flavour modifiers in cocktails.

Keep refrigerated and use within 1 month.

Makes: 1 cup

½ cup fresh **raspberries**

1 cup **sugar**

½ cup **water**

1 Muddle the raspberries and cover with sugar to macerate for 30 minutes.

2 Heat the water (don't boil) and add the raspberry mixture.

3 Stir until the sugar has dissolved.

4 Strain the mixture and let cool before bottling.

ORGEAT
(ALMOND SYRUP)

A staple ingredient in tropical drinks, orgeat is essentially sweetened almond milk. For a quick hack, use store bought unsweetened almond milk and sweeten it. Otherwise, make your own almond milk by blending blanched almonds with water.

Keep refrigerated and use within 2 weeks.

Makes: 1⅔ cups

2 cups **blanched almonds**

1¼ cups **water**

1½ cups **superfine sugar**

½ tsp **orange blossom water**

1 oz (30ml) **brandy**

1 In a food processor or high-speed blender, blend the almonds and water until a paste forms.

2 In a saucepan, combine the almond paste and sugar. Place over medium-low heat and stir until the sugar has dissolved.

3 Remove from the heat and let sit at room temperature for 4 to 8 hours.

4 Strain through a cheesecloth and discard the solids.

5 Add the orange blossom water and brandy before bottling.

GRENADINE
(POMEGRANATE SYRUP)

Avoid store-bought grenadine, as most brands are not true representations of a vibrant and brightly flavoured pomegranate syrup that you want to use in your drinks.

Keep refrigerated and use within 2 weeks.

Makes: 1⅔ cups

1 cup **pomegranate juice**

1¼ cups **superfine sugar**

½ tsp **pomegranate molasses** (optional)

¼ tsp **rose water** (optional)

1 In a saucepan, heat the pomegranate juice, sugar, and pomegranate molasses (if using) over medium-low heat until the sugar is dissolved.

2 Remove from the heat and let cool. Add the rose water (if using) before bottling.

CREAM OF COCONUT

Coco Lopez cream of coconut is the commercial product of choice for many bars around the world but it can be difficult to source in some countries outside the United States. Jeff "Beachbum" Berry has stated that Coco Lopez is the best for cocktails.

This DIY recipe avoids all the emulsifiers, stabilisers, and growth-inhibiting agents for a more natural cream of coconut. It has a shorter shelf life, but once you taste a Painkiller made with the homemade version, it won't last long at all.

Keep refrigerated and use within 2 weeks.

Makes: 2 cups

1⅔ cups **coconut milk**

1¾ cups **sugar**

Pinch of **salt**

1 In a saucepan, combine all the ingredients. Place over low heat and stir until the sugar is dissolved. (The colour will change from white to partially transparent.)

2 Let cool before bottling.

OLEO-SACCHARUM

Often referred to as "oleo," the name of this intense lemon syrup translates to "oil sugar." Sugar extracts the lemon oils from the rind, leaving the acidity of the flesh behind. The resulting syrup can be used to make incredible punches.

Keep refrigerated and use within 2 weeks.

Makes: ¾ cup

4 **lemons**

1 cup **sugar**

1 Using a vegetable peeler, peel the lemons. Place the peels in a bowl and cover with the sugar. (The peeled lemons can be reserved for juicing.)

2 Muddle to bruise the peel and initiate the process.

3 Cover and let sit overnight until the sugar has dissolved. Alternatively, use a vacuum bag to expedite and improve the process.

4 Strain and transfer to a bottle.

LIME CORDIAL

Lime cordial plays a significant role in the Gimlet. This recipe can be used as a substitute for Rose's Sweetened Lime Juice.

Keep refrigerated and use within 2 weeks.

Makes: 1½ cups

1½ cups **simple syrup** (page 26)

3 tsp **citric acid**

4 tsp **lime zest**

1½ oz (45ml) freshly squeezed **lime juice**

1 In a food processor, blend all ingredients until well combined.

2 Strain through a fine strainer or cheesecloth.

3 Transfer to a bottle.

GINGER BEER

Making ginger beer is surprisingly simple and the best part is it can be tailored to your liking. Adjust the ginger to change the spiciness or alter the amount of sugar to adjust the sweetness. This uncarbonated version is best suited for the **Gin Gin Mule** (page 147).

Keep refrigerated and use within 3 days.

Makes: 4 cups

4 cups **water**

4 oz (110g) finely grated **ginger**

2 tbsp **brown sugar**

½ oz (15ml) freshly squeezed **lime juice**

1 In a small saucepan, bring the water to a boil. Turn off the heat and add the ginger. Cool for 1 hour.

2 Strain with a cheesecloth (the resulting liquid will be cloudy). Discard the ginger solids. To the ginger liquid, add the brown sugar and lime juice.

3 Transfer to a bottle.

OTHER INGREDIENTS

ICE

The majority of mixed drinks are composed of 25 to 35 percent water via dilution, yet ice is an often overlooked ingredient in cocktails. Always use the best-quality ingredients at your disposal, which includes the type of ice you use to make drinks. Shared freezer space can impart unwanted flavours on ice so it's recommended to cover ice trays if making ice at home.

Cubed ice ¾- to 1¼-inch (20–30mm) cubes are ideal for stirring and shaking cocktails. For spirit-forward drinks served on the rocks, 2-inch (50mm) cubes are preferred.

Crushed or pebble ice Small ice increases surface area for faster chilling. It's best used in tropical drinks that contain multiple and potentially high-proof rums.

Clear ice A large, clear block of ice is great for chilling punches, or it can be cut into smaller cubes for drinks served on the rocks. You can make large, clear blocks at home with the "cooler method," which uses directional freezing to separate gases and impurities from the ice. Fill a small cooler halfway with water and place it in the freezer with the lid off. This forces the ice to freeze from top down, pushing the gases to the bottom of the block and leaving a clear block of ice at the top. (Further information about this method can be found online.)

GARNISHES

In some circumstances a garnish is purely decorative but more often than not a cocktail garnish plays a special role in finishing and elevating a drink. Even a seemingly simple twist of orange will extract the fragrant essential oils from the fruit's skin, enhancing the aromatics and adding a layer of complexity to a drink. The following garnishes will amplify your drinks aesthetically whilst providing additional flavour and aroma.

Lemons and limes will keep in the fridge in a sealed container for up to a month.

Oranges are mostly used for the peel and expressing oils over a cocktail. Firm, fresh fruit is preferred for easier peeling.

Maraschino cherries are candied cherries in a thick, rich syrup that have an almost indefinite shelf life. Luxardo is my preferred brand. (Avoid the bright red varieties!)

Mint should be stored in a sealed container with a moist paper towel for maximum freshness. Its aroma will begin to fade after a couple of days, so make those Mojitos whilst it's fresh.

Green olives are essential if you enjoy the occasional martini. Make sure you opt for brined olives.

Pineapple wedges and the spears are great for garnishing tropical drinks. Store the pineapple spears in a sealed container in the freezer for a quick and easy tropical garnish that will last a long time.

Cucumber can be muddled, sliced into wheels, or peeled into long ribbons for garnishing.

Nutmeg adds a warming aroma to flips, nogs, and numerous tropical cocktails. Be sure to use freshly grated nutmeg for the best flavour.

CITRUS

Lemons and limes are an essential ingredient in a long list of cocktails, but they can be expensive and a huge cause of waste in bars. Bartenders have long been experimenting with citrus replacements in an effort to minimise waste and become more sustainable.

A revolutionary technique to extend citrus juice yields called "super juice" has become popular amongst the bar community. It uses citric and malic acids, which are readily available at some health food stores and most brew shops. The finished juice is almost indistinguishable from fresh citrus juice and can be used in any recipe calling for freshly squeezed juice. Keep refrigerated and use within one week.

SUPER LIME JUICE

1 organic **lime**

Citric acid (0.66 x weight of the lime peels)

Malic acid (0.33 x weight of the lime peels)

SUPER LEMON JUICE

1 organic **lemon**

Citric acid (equal to weight of the lemon peels)

1 Peel the lemon or lime. Weigh the peel (take note of the weight) and place it in a jar.

2 Add the appropriate amounts of acid(s) according to the relevant formula. Let the mixture rest for 1 to 2 hours, until oils are extracted and a liquid has formed.

3 Add water in an amount of 16.66 times the weight of the peels.

4 Juice the peeled citrus and add the juice to the jar.

5 Transfer to a blender. Blend for 30 seconds.

6 Strain through a cheesecloth into a sterilised bottle.

BAR TOOLS + EQUIPMENT

ESSENTIAL TOOLS

These are the eight bar tools that are the bare essentials required to mix cocktails. You may already have alternatives you can use, such as a knife or chopstick for stirring if you're in a bind, but having the right tools makes preparing drinks a little easier and more enjoyable.

Cocktail shaker
I recommend a tin on tin shaker set consisting of a small 18-ounce tin and a larger 28-ounce tin. This type of shaker is a workhorse, inexpensive, durable, easy to separate, and has better thermal conductivity than glass.

Jigger I prefer using a double-sided (1-oz/2-oz) Japanese-style jigger with inner markings. The internal markings are useful for smaller measurements (¼ oz, ½ oz, ¾ oz, etc.) and the tall, slim design is forgiving when measuring.

Bar spoon A 12-inch (30cm) bar spoon is a comfortable length for stirring, unless you have a rather tall mixing glass, in which case a 15¾-inch (40cm) bar spoon will be better suited. I prefer a weighted teardrop-style bar spoon for balance, although spoons with a flat disk are useful for crushing sugar cubes.

Hawthorne strainer Used to strain a finished drink from a cocktail shaker (or mixing glass), separating the drink from the ice used to chill it.

Paring knife Necessary for cutting citrus and other fruit and preparing garnishes.

Chopping board Protect your countertop when cutting fruit and garnishes.

Citrus press or juicer
The citrus press is best suited for pressing lemons and limes on the spot although large citrus will not fit in the average-sized citrus press. A citrus juicer is ideal for all citrus and bigger volumes when preparing juices ahead of time.

Ice cube moulds Tovolo makes the ideal silicone ice moulds that produce 15 (1¼-in; 30mm) cubes perfect for making cocktails. These cubes can also be broken down to be used as crushed ice.

Scan to see Steve's equipment recommendations.

RECOMMENDED TOOLS

These tools are recommended additions to your barware collection but aren't necessary when first getting started. This list is sorted by my recommended purchase order.

Mixing glass A vessel for making stirred drinks. It didn't make the essentials list as it can potentially be replaced with a shaker tin. A 500-millilitre glass is an ideal size.

Peeler The two best peelers for citrus peel garnishes are the OXO Y peeler (it's sharp—use with caution!) or a Boska cheese slicer.

Fine strainer This helps to remove particles such as pips, pulp, and ice shards that may pass through a Hawthorne strainer.

Muddler If you love making juleps, mojitos, or caipirinhas then a muddler is required.

Microplane Mostly used for grating nutmeg over the top of tropical drinks, flips, and nogs.

Funnel Makes life easier when you're transferring syrups and ingredients into bottles.

Serrated bread knife If you make clear block ice in your freezer, a 9-inch (23cm) serrated knife is a useful tool to break down the ice into smaller blocks.

Mallet Used with a serrated knife for cutting ice. After scoring the ice, a gentle tap on the back of the knife with a mallet will split the ice in two. Also used with a Lewis bag to produce crushed ice.

Lewis bag A small cotton drawstring bag used to hold ice whilst it's being crushed with a mallet (or muddler).

Julep strainer The julep strainer is a nice item to have in your collection but it can be replaced with a Hawthorne strainer.

EQUIPMENT

The following two pieces of equipment are by no means necessary but are certainly handy to have.

Milkshake maker Also called a drink mixer, this small appliance has a spindle blender that mixes rather than pulverising the ice. A short blend for 3 or 4 seconds, known as flash blending, will chill, dilute, and aerate a drink with minimum effort at incredible speed. These mixers are relatively inexpensive and I highly recommend getting one.

Blender I reserve my blender for making orgeat (page 28) and "super juice" (page 31), as I rarely make frozen drinks. If you love frozen margaritas and daiquiris then get the best quality blender you can afford. Ice is an extremely hard ingredient so crush it before adding it to your blender to save your blender blades.

GLASSWARE

ESSENTIAL GLASSWARE

There is an abundance of glassware that you can opt for to improve the presentation of your cocktails, but these are the absolute essentials for mixed drinks.

Old fashioned
A traditional old-fashioned glass holds approximately 6 to 9 ounces (180–270ml) and was popular in the nineteenth century. Glassware sizes increased, and by the early twentieth century the double old-fashioned glass was the standard, holding approximately 12 to 16 ounces (360–480ml). Most commonly used for serving drinks on the rocks (over ice), including old fashioneds, caipirinhas, margaritas, etc.

Coupe Coupe glasses can vary dramatically in size. A standard, inexpensive coupe that I recommend is the Libbey Embassy coupe, which is 5½ ounces (165ml). Spiegelau and Riedel make a very nice range of coupes as well as other cocktail glasses. Used for serving drinks "up" (in a stemmed glass with no ice).

Highball The highball glass was introduced in the 1890s and bridged the gap between the smaller Fizz glass and the larger Collins glass. A typical highball glass has a capacity of 8 to 12 ounces (240–360ml) and is commonly used for two-ingredient mixed drinks known as highballs and other "tall" drinks such as the Mojito. This glass quickly became a one-size-fits-all replacement for the Fizz and Collins glasses.

Nick and Nora Dale DeGroff reintroduced this 1930s-style glass at the Rainbow Room in 1987 and his protegé Audrey Saunders used it at her bar, Pegu Club, from 2005. It is my favourite glass to use for spirit-forward cocktails served up despite its small 5-ounce (150ml) capacity.

Hurricane glass This large 20-ounce (600ml) tulip-style glass is used to serve the Hurricane at Pat O'Brien's Bar in New Orleans and can be used for tropical drinks such as the Piña Colada.

Pilsner glass Traditionally used as a beer glass, but it also doubles as a great cocktail glass for swizzles and tropical drinks served over crushed or pebble ice.

Brandy balloon Traditionally used as a cognac glass and also known as a snifter. The shape of the glass is designed to increase the surface area of the spirit and encapsulate the aromas, whilst the rounded bottom allows the glass to be cupped in the hand. This glass is a great alternative for tropical cocktails served on crushed or pebble ice such as the Brancolada.

Fizz or **Collins** These glasses were introduced in the late nineteenth century and designed to serve carbonated drinks. They are tall and narrow in order to maintain carbonation. The **Fizz** glass has a capacity of 6 ounces (180ml) and is suitable for carbonated drinks served without ice, whilst the **Collins** glass has a capacity of 10 to 14 ounces (300–420ml) and is suitable for carbonated drinks served with ice.

Flute A flute is typically used for serving champagne so I reserve this for cocktails containing champagne or prosecco.

TECHNIQUES

SHAKING

Shaking a cocktail is the most efficient manual method of chilling and diluting a drink. It quickly approaches thermal equilibrium within 10 seconds. Continued shaking beyond this point will have very little effect on chilling and dilution.

The technique of shaking a cocktail also adds texture to a drink as the movement of the ice introduces tiny air bubbles. The air begins to escape the moment the drink is served, so a shaken drink is best consumed immediately after serving.

When shaking a drink, the ideal size for ice cubes is ¾ inch (20mm) to 1¼ inches (30mm). The specific shaking technique used has minimal effect on the finished drink as long as you agitate the ice from end to end within the shaker and you shake for 10 to 12 seconds. Shaken drinks are typically served at approximately 23°F (-5°C).

Dry shake is the term for shaking a drink without ice. This is a common technique used to emulsify eggs prior to shaking with ice. Reverse dry shaking is when dry shaking follows the wet shake rather than preceding it.

Wet shake is the term used when shaking with ice. The term is usually only specified in a recipe when in conjunction with a dry shake.

Whip shake is often used for tropical drinks that are served over crushed or pebble ice. It is a short shake with a little pebble ice, which will chill slightly, combine the ingredients, and add texture through aeration.

HOW TO SHAKE A COCKTAIL

1   In a shaker tin (or Boston glass), combine the ingredients.

2   Add ice (about ½ cup).

3   Combine the two tins and firmly tap the small tin to seal the shaker.

4   Find a comfortable position to hold both tins, holding the small tin closest to you with your dominant hand and the larger tin with the other hand.

5   Shake back and forth with a subtle circular motion, agitating the ice from one end to the other for 10 to 12 seconds.

6   Separate the shaker by pushing the small tin away. If the tins are firmly joined, find the point at which both tins meet then tap a quarter-turn away from this point ensuring to hold both tins.

7   Use a Hawthorne strainer to strain into your glass.

STIRRING

Compared to shaking, stirring is a far less efficient method of chilling and diluting a drink. It would take over two minutes of stirring for the temperature of the drink to plateau.

The size of the ice, the speed of stirring, and the length of time that you stir all play a part in the finished drink, so it requires more practice to achieve consistency.

To find your ideal stirring time and technique, start by stirring a spirit-forward drink such as a Manhattan with a digital thermometer probe whilst timing and counting the revolutions required to reach 28°F (-2°C). Taste test and rerun the test with different final temperatures until you find your preferred drink. Once you're satisfied with the finished drink, you will know the time required to stir most spirit-forward drinks. Your drinks will remain consistent as long as you use the same sized ice and maintain the same stirring speed. Some drinks will be better at different temperatures and dilution but this is a good starting point for making stirred drinks that are served up. Stirred drinks that are served over ice can be served underdiluted as the drink will dilute further in the glass.

IDEAL TEMPERATURE RANGES FOR STIRRED DRINKS

Served without ice	25°F to 32°F (-4 to 0°C)
Served over ice	32°F to 36°F (0 to 2°C)

Timing and counting revolutions are simply a guide to help you make consistent drinks. Taste testing is recommended to ensure consistency.

Prefer to skip the testing? I like my Manhattans served between 28°F (-1°C) and 30°F (-2°C), which takes me 22 to 30 seconds and 60 to 80 revolutions to achieve with 1-inch (25mm) ice cubes and a mixing glass straight from the freezer.

HOW TO STIR A COCKTAIL

1   In a mixing glass, combine the ingredients.

2   Add plenty of ice, enough to sit above the level of the liquid. (The mixing glass should be half to three-quarters full of ice.)

3   Hold the bar spoon between your middle and ring finger, securing in position with your thumb.

4   Stir at a steady pace whilst holding the base of the mixing glass with the other hand. The back of the spoon should be against the mixing glass as you stir.

5   Stir until the ideal temperature and dilution is reached, about 15 to 30 seconds.

6   Use a Hawthorne or julep strainer to strain into a chilled cocktail glass.

TECHNIQUES

STRAINING

Now that we have most of the technical side of making a cocktail, here comes the easy part. Straining the drink into the glass. There are several types of strainers including the julep, Hawthorne, and fine strainer.

Julep strainers are designed to sit inside the glass and are most commonly used for spirit-forward stirred drinks made within a mixing glass. Its purpose is to hold back the ice whilst the liquid is transferred into the cocktail glass. Find a julep strainer with a small kink in the neck, which is ideal for resting on the edge of the mixing glass, making it easier to strain single-handedly.

Hawthorne strainers are designed to sit on top of the cocktail shaker with the coil of the strainer facing into the tin. Pressing the Hawthorne strainer against the lip of the tin will "close the gate," tightening the coils and result in a finer strain. The coil of the Hawthorne strainer can be added into a cocktail shaker when using egg whites for additional aeration and a thicker foam. It can also be used as a julep strainer replacement when straining from a mixing glass.

Fine strainers are used in conjunction with a Hawthorne strainer. This is commonly referred to as double straining and is a technique used to ensure small ice shards and particles do not end up in the finished drink.

MUDDLING

An important technique for making Caipirinhas and Smashes. Muddling fresh lime wedges, for example, extracts both the fresh citrus juice and the oils from the skin resulting in a more complex lime flavour. When muddling soft herbs such as basil or mint, a gentler hand is required to only bruise the herbs and extract the aromatics— a heavy hand will result in extracting unwanted vegetal flavours.

ADDING A SALT OR SUGAR RIM

A seasoned rim on a glass adds an additional layer of flavour. Start by moistening the outer rim of the glass with a wedge of lemon or lime before rotating the glass in a shallow bowl of salt or sugar. Gently tap the glass to remove any excess.

CHILLING AND DILUTION

Chilling and dilution are directly linked to one another. To compare the effects of different sized ice and stirring techniques, make several Manhattans using different sized ice. Stir the drinks with a digital thermometer probe and vary the speed of stirring. You will discover that each drink will require a different stirring time, but as long as you cease stirring once the drink reaches the same temperature (e.g., 28°F/-2°C), the amount of dilution will be identical, demonstrating the correlation between chilling and dilution.

The key difference between the cubed, pebble, and block ice is their surface area. Smaller ice has a larger surface area in relation to its volume. Ice melts at its surface so increasing the surface area results in faster chilling as well as faster dilution.

It's worth noting that ice sitting within a drink doesn't chill a drink quickly. Stirring or shaking increases contact between the ice and liquid therefore increasing the rate at which it chills. The more movement, the quicker the drink can chill which is why shaking a cocktail is so efficient.

BALANCING COCKTAILS

Great cocktails require a balance of flavour, strength, and acidity, although acidity of a cocktail is what is most commonly referred to when "balance" is mentioned.

The sour family of cocktails encompasses an enormous variety of drinks and is the ideal starting point when learning about balancing acidity in a drink. A common sour formula is 2 ounces (60ml) base spirit, ¾ ounce (22.5ml) sweet, and ¾ ounce (22.5ml) sour, but tastes are subjective so some people may find this balanced whilst others may find it sweet. The best method to find your preferred sour ratio, and to understand balancing acidity in cocktails, is by doing a taste comparison of different daiquiri ratios side by side.

Here are some preferred ratios of renowned professional bartenders that I recommend comparing:

BARTENDER	RUM	LIME JUICE	SIMPLE SYRUP	MY THOUGHTS
Ryan Chetiyawardana	2 oz (60ml)	⅔ oz (20ml)	½ oz (15ml)	Balanced
Jim Meehan	2 oz (60ml)	¾ oz (22.5ml)	¾ oz (22.5ml)	Slightly sweeter
Sasha Petraske	2 oz (60ml)	⅞ oz (26ml)	¾ oz (22.5ml)	More acidic

TECHNIQUES

FLOATING

When using this technique, the final ingredient is added slowly and carefully so that it "floats" on the surface with minimal mixing. Drinks served over ice with a float only require a gentle hand and a slow pour. Other drinks may require a little more technique and care, such as the Dominicana, which calls for a heavy cream float. In such cases, use the bowl of a bar spoon to catch the ingredient and slow the flow at the surface of the drink to create the ideal definition between ingredients.

FLAMED ZEST

Dale DeGroff popularised the flamed orange zest when he used it to finish off his Cosmopolitans.

1 To flame a zest, cut a disk of orange approximately 1-inch (2.5cm) in diameter, ensuring there is some pith but no flesh from the fruit.

2 Ignite a match and let it burn for a few seconds until the sulphur subsides.

3 Gently heat the surface of the orange peel for 1 to 2 seconds.

4 Hold the lit match 2 inches (5cm) away from the orange peel before squeezing the disk and expressing the oils through the flame and over the drink. The oils should ignite and add a pleasant burnt orange note to your cocktail.

FAT-WASHING

This technique involves infusing flavours from ingredients containing fat into spirits, ingredients such as bacon, coconut oil, and butter.

1 Heat your choice of fat until it melts.

2 In a lidded container, combine the fat with your choice of spirit (about 1½ oz [45ml] of fat per 750ml bottle).

3 Let infuse for 3 to 4 hours.

4 Place in the freezer for 2 to 3 hours.

5 Remove the solid fat from the top of the liquid.

6 Strain through a cheesecloth.

7 Bottle and store in the fridge.

CREATING A SIGNATURE COCKTAIL

MR. POTATO HEAD

The term *Mr. Potato Head* is used when substituting an ingredient or multiple ingredients into a cocktail template and was coined by Death & Co's Phil Ward.

A simple substitution or two in a cocktail can result in an entirely different drink and it is a common practice for creating new drinks. The Negroni, for example, calls for gin, Campari, and sweet vermouth yet substituting the gin with a funky Jamaican rum (Smith & Cross) results in a rich, funky almost chocolate-y variation on the classic Negroni, called the Kingston Negroni.

Try using this technique with some of your favourite cocktails, substituting the spirit, juice, bitters, and/or modifiers to create your own signature drink.

SPLITTING INGREDIENTS

Using a combination of rums to add complexity is common practice when making tropical drinks, and it's a great technique for other mixed drinks too. The **Conquistador** (page 244) by Sam Ross is a good example of this. It's a sour cocktail with a split-spirit base (rum and blanco tequila) and split citrus (lemon and lime juice). Not all spirits work well with one another, so experimentation is key.

SPIRIT AND FLAVOUR COMBINATIONS

Classic flavour pairings are a great place to start when planning your own signature cocktail as they will create a solid foundation for developing drinks.

SPIRIT	OTHER LIQUOR	FRUIT & HERBS
Whiskey	absinthe, Angostura bitters, Amaro Averna, Campari, cognac, Cynar, maraschino liqueur, orange bitters, St-Germain, sweet vermouth	apple, cacao, chamomile, cherry, cinnamon, coffee, figs, ginger, grapefruit, honey, lemon, lime, mint, peach, pear, pineapple
Gin	absinthe, Aperol, apricot brandy liqueur, Campari, champagne, Chartreuse, Cynar, dry sherry, dry vermouth, Earl Grey tea, Italicus, orange liqueur, sweet vermouth, St-Germain	basil, celery, cucumber, ginger, honey, lemon, lime, mint, orange, peach, raspberry, strawberry
Rum	allspice dram, cognac, orange liqueurs, other rums, Velvet falernum	almonds (orgeat), cinnamon, coconut, coffee, demerara sugar, ginger, grapefruit, honey, lime, maple syrup, mint, orange, passionfruit, pineapple, pomegranate (grenadine), vanilla
Tequila / Mezcal	Aperol, orange liqueur, Yellow Chartreuse	agave syrup, black pepper, cinnamon, grapefruit, jalapeño, lime, mango, orange, pineapple, sage, strawberry

COCKTAIL MENUS

When entertaining, preparing drinks for guests can quickly become overwhelming. I've created a few simple menus centred around a single spirit. These menus make for easy entertaining and a shorter shopping list, which means you won't blow your budget.

WHISKEY COCKTAILS

A whiskey-focused menu that covers all bases—vermouth, bitter, spirit-forward, and sour cocktails to keep guests happy.

COCKTAILS	SHOPPING LIST
Boulevardier (page 60)	Bourbon whiskey
Gold Rush (page 71)	Rye whiskey
Manhattan (page 80)	Campari
Old Fashioned (page 88)	Sweet vermouth
Whiskey Smash (page 112)	Angostura bitters
Whiskey Sour (page 115)	Orange bitters
	Honey syrup (page 29)
	Simple syrup (page 28)
	Eggs
	Lemons
	Oranges
	Mint

RUM COCKTAILS

Start the evening on Mojitos, Mai Tais, and Daiquiris, and then finish with a Dominicana for a decadent nightcap.

COCKTAILS	SHOPPING LIST
Daiquiri (page 200)	Aged rum
Dominicana (page 203)	Lightly aged rum
Cable Car (page 195)	Spiced rum
Mai Tai (page 215)	Coffee liqueur
Mojito (page 216)	Orange liqueur (Cointreau, dry curaçao, etc.)
	Orgeat (page 30)
	Simple syrup (page 28)
	Cinnamon sugar
	Heavy cream
	Lemons
	Limes
	Mint
	Soda water

GIN COCKTAILS

This extensive menu of gin cocktails has only a few bottles on the shopping list. Spend some time preparing your syrups in advance for a fuss-free evening sipping Clover Clubs, Gin Gin Mules, and Martinis.

COCKTAILS	SHOPPING LIST
Bees Knees (page 120)	Gin
Cosmonaut (page 131)	Campari
Clover Club (page 127)	Cointreau
Gimlet (page 140)	Sweet vermouth
Gin Gin Mule (page 147)	Dry vermouth
Martini (page 159)	Orange bitters
Negroni (page 160)	Honey syrup (page 29)
Southside (page 172)	Lime cordial (page 30)
White Lady (page 180)	Raspberry syrup (page 29)
	Simple syrup (page 28)
	Ginger beer (page 31)
	Eggs
	Lemons
	Limes
	Mint
	Oranges
	Raspberry jam

TEQUILA / MEZCAL COCKTAILS

The ultimate poolside party menu featuring Margaritas and refreshing Palomas. This limited menu is perfectly suited for summer entertaining.

COCKTAILS	SHOPPING LIST
Dead Man's Handle (page 247)	Blanco tequila
Margarita (page 251)	Reposado tequila
Oaxaca Old Fashioned (page 255)	Mezcal
Paloma (page 256)	Aperol
Tommy's Margarita (page 259)	Cointreau
	Angostura bitters
	Orgeat (page 30)
	Agave syrup
	Grapefruit soda
	Limes
	Oranges
	Salt
	Tajin (chili and lime seasoning)

THE COCKTAILS

A few things to note . . .

It's common practice to measure the least expensive ingredient first in case of error.

Always add the ice to your shaker or mixing glass after you build the drink in case you get distracted and can't finish making the drink immediately.

After measuring viscous ingredients, such as honey syrup, reuse the jigger to measure the remaining ingredients for the drink. This will ensure that all the viscous ingredient is used and the jigger is rinsed for the next drink.

Glassware should almost always be chilled. If you don't have the fridge or freezer space, prechill the glass with ice.

Unless otherwise stated, you can make the following assumptions:

- All juice is fresh and double-strained
- Cream is heavy
- Herbs are fresh
- Milk is whole
- Sugar is granulated

Every recipe is accompanied by a short video. To access the video, scan the QR code with your mobile phone.

ORIGINATED	TYPE	METHOD	GLASSWARE	GARNISH
1860s	Highball	Built	Highball glass	Orange slice

AMERICANO

The bright red, bitter liqueur Campari was created by Italian bartender Gaspare Campari in 1860. Shortly after, he tried mixing sweet vermouth with his bitter liqueur. He called the drink the "Milano-Torino" to pay tribute to the origins of its ingredients: Campari from Milan and vermouth from Turin.

Bartenders at Gaspare's bar began adding soda water to the drink, and it became popular with American expats around the time of prohibition, resulting in the name Americano. The Milano-Torino also led to the creation of the **Negroni** (page 160).

1 oz (30ml) **Campari**

1 oz (30ml) **sweet vermouth**

2½ oz (75ml) **soda water**

1 Fill a highball glass with ice and add all ingredients.

2 Gently stir to combine.

3 Garnish with a slice of orange.

Yet to acquire the bittersweet taste of Campari? Ease into it with two of my favourites, the **Enzoni** *(page 136) or the* **Garibaldi** *(page 51).*

ORIGINATED	TYPE	METHOD	GLASSWARE	GARNISH
1970s	Highball	Blended	Highball glass	Orange wedge

GARIBALDI

Military general Giuseppe Garibaldi was a central figure in the Italian military and is credited with playing a significant role in the unification and liberation of Italy in the mid-1800s. Soldiers under Garibaldi's command wore bright reddish-orange shirts that matched the color of this drink, giving the Garibaldi its name.

The Campari brand pushed the combination of Campari and orange juice in the 1970s, but it fell into obscurity until the New York cocktail bar Dante revived it in 2015. The team used a Breville juicer to give the drink its signature fluffy texture.

The Garibaldi consists of just two ingredients, so the key to elevating the drink is technique. Fresh juice is the only option, and blending or whip shaking is the best way to aerate the drink for a great, fluffy Garibaldi.

1½ oz (45ml) **Campari**

4 oz (120ml) freshly squeezed **orange juice**

1 In a milkshake maker tin, combine the ingredients.

2 Add ice and flash blend.

3 Strain over ice into a highball glass and garnish with an orange wedge.

Try a Garibaldi with another variety of juice such as pineapple or grapefruit.

If you don't have a milkshake maker, you can whip shake this drink. (See page 38.)

ORIGINATED	TYPE	METHOD	GLASSWARE	GARNISH
1800s	Miscellaneous	Built	Wine glass	Orange wheel

VENETIAN SPRITZ

In the 1800s, many Austrians didn't enjoy the acidic Italian wine from Northern Italy, so they added a *spritzen* of carbonated water to lighten the flavour. This evolved into the Venetian Spritz, which incorporates a bittersweet Italian liqueur.

Although Select Aperitivo was the original liqueur of choice for the Venetian Spritz, the Campari Group began to push Aperol in global marketing campaigns, and it soon became the go-to liqueur for a Spritz. Compare Select, Aperol, Campari, and Cynar to find out which is your preferred aperitif.

2 oz (60ml) **Select Aperitivo**

3 oz (90ml) **prosecco**

1 oz (30ml) **soda water**

1 Fill a large wine glass with ice and add all the ingredients.

2 Give a gentle stir to combine.

3 Garnish with a slice of orange.

Many people like to garnish a Spritz with skewered olives. Salt suppresses bitter notes and enhances the perceived sweetness, so briny olives will alter the drinking experience.

ORIGINATED	TYPE	METHOD	GLASSWARE	GARNISH
2006	Vermouth cocktail	Stirred	Coupe glass	None

BENSONHURST

The Bensonhurst is one of several variations on the **Brooklyn** (page 63). Chad Solomon created it in 2006, while he was working at both Milk & Honey and Pegu Club. Lacking the original-formula Amer Picon that is called for in the Brooklyn, he used Cynar instead.

2 oz (60ml) **rye whiskey** (Rittenhouse recommended)

1 oz (30ml) **dry vermouth** (Dolin recommended)

⅓ oz (10ml) **maraschino liqueur** (Luxardo recommended)

1 tsp (5ml) **Cynar**

1 In a mixing glass, combine all ingredients.

2 Add ice and stir for 15 to 30 seconds.

3 Strain into a chilled coupe glass.

*Enjoy the Bensonhurst? Other variations on the Brooklyn named for Brooklyn neighbourhoods include the **Red Hook** (page 96) and the **Cobble Hill** (page 67).*

ORIGINATED	TYPE	METHOD	GLASSWARE	GARNISH
2007	Cocktail	Stirred	Old-fashioned glass	Orange twist

BENTON'S OLD FASHIONED

Don Lee, former bartender at the New York bar PDT, loved experimenting with a technique known as fat-washing, in which fat is used to flavour spirits. Don fell in love with Benton's Country Farm smoky bacon from Tennessee, so he incorporated the streaky bacon into a variation on the **Old Fashioned** (page 88). His experiments and the Benton's Old Fashioned kickstarted the fat-washing trend, which is still used in bars today.

2 oz (60ml) **bacon fat-washed bourbon whiskey** (see note)

¼ oz (7.5ml) **maple syrup**

2 dashes of **Angostura bitters**

1   In a mixing glass, combine all ingredients.

2   Add ice and stir for 15 to 30 seconds.

3   Strain over a large ice cube into an old-fashioned glass.

4   Garnish with an orange twist.

Don prefers Four Roses bourbon whiskey for this drink.

Experiment with fat-washed spirits using bacon fat, butter, or coconut oil. Refer to page 42 to learn more about the fat-washing technique.

ORIGINATED	TYPE	METHOD	GLASSWARE	GARNISH
2005	Vermouth cocktail	Stirred	Coupe glass	Maraschino cherry

BLACK MANHATTAN

The Black Manhattan was created in 2005 by Todd Smith, a bartender at Bourbon & Branch in San Francisco. This variation on a classic **Manhattan** (page 80) calls for replacing the sweet vermouth with Amaro Averna, resulting in complex herbal notes.

2 oz (60ml) **rye whiskey**

1 oz (30ml) **Averna amaro**

1 dash of **Angostura bitters**

1 dash of **orange bitters**

1   In a mixing glass, combine all ingredients.

2   Add ice and stir for 15 to 30 seconds.

3   Strain into a chilled coupe glass.

4   Garnish with a maraschino cherry.

Don't have Averna? Experiment with another amaro in the Manhattan recipe format.

ORIGINATED	TYPE	METHOD	GLASSWARE	GARNISH
Circa 1927	Vermouth cocktail	Stirred	Old-fashioned glass	Orange twist

BOULEVARDIER

The Boulevardier first appeared in print in Harry McElhone's *Barflies and Cocktails*. It wasn't featured in the list of drink recipes, but was mentioned in a brief article that implied the drink was created by Erskine Gwynne. He was a regular at Harry's New York Bar in Paris and an editor at a monthly magazine named *The Boulevardier,* hence the drink's name.

The original recipe called for equal parts bourbon whiskey, Campari, and sweet vermouth, but over the last decade, many bartenders have shown preference for rye whiskey in a slightly higher ratio.

1¼ oz (37.5ml) **bourbon whiskey**

1 oz (30ml) **Campari**

1 oz (30ml) **sweet vermouth**

1   In a mixing glass, combine all the ingredients.

2   Add ice and stir for 15 to 30 seconds.

3   Strain over a large ice cube into an old-fashioned glass.

4   Garnish with a twist of orange.

Sticking with the classic equal-parts recipe? Consider using a 100-proof whiskey.

For a spicier Boulevardier, try using rye whiskey.

ORIGINATED	TYPE	METHOD	GLASSWARE	GARNISH
1908	Vermouth cocktail	Stirred	Coupe glass	None

BROOKLYN

The Brooklyn cocktail was first published in Jacob Grohusko's 1908 *Jack's Manual* and is most commonly made with dry vermouth despite the original recipe calling for sweet vermouth. This is perhaps due to an alternative version that appeared in Jacques Straub's *Manual of Mixed Drinks* just five years later, which called—perhaps mistakenly—for dry vermouth.

This is the original version published in 1908. Amer Picon isn't readily available in many countries outside of France, so you may need to substitute. The most common substitutes are CioCiaro or Ramazzotti, both with a dash of orange bitters. Finally, you may want to adjust the ratios to suit a less sweet, modern palate (e.g., 2 ounces rye whiskey, ½ ounce sweet vermouth, ¼ ounce amaro of choice, and ¼ ounce maraschino liqueur).

1½ oz (45ml) **rye whiskey**

1½ oz (45ml) **sweet vermouth**

1 dash of **Amer Picon**

1 dash of **maraschino liqueur**

1 In a mixing glass, combine all the ingredients.

2 Add ice and stir for 15 to 30 seconds.

3 Strain into a chilled coupe glass.

Want to try your hand at a DIY Amer Picon? A copycat recipe for Amer Picon called Amer Boudreau can be found online.

Consider garnishing with a lemon twist if you decide to use CioCiaro or Ramazzotti.

ORIGINATED	TYPE	METHOD	GLASSWARE	GARNISH
1930s	Sour	Shaken	Coupe glass	None

BROWN DERBY

Like many classic cocktails, the Brown Derby has an elusive and much-debated background. The most well-known version of the drink is made with bourbon and originated in the 1930s at the Vendome Club in Hollywood. It is named after the Brown Derby restaurant, a famous hat-shaped diner located near the Vendome.

An alternative version, which is definitely worth trying, is essentially a Jamaican rum daiquiri with maple sugar (or syrup) as the sweetener. It calls for 2 ounces (60ml) dark Jamaican rum, 1 ounce (30ml) lime juice, and 1 teaspoon maple sugar or maple syrup.

2 oz (60ml) **bourbon whiskey**

1 oz (30ml) freshly squeezed
  grapefruit juice

¾ oz (22.5ml) **honey syrup**
  (page 29)

1 In a cocktail shaker, combine all ingredients.

2 Add ice and shake for 10 to 12 seconds.

3 Double strain into a chilled coupe glass.

Try a side-by-side comparison of the two different versions to find your favourite.

ORIGINATED	TYPE	METHOD	GLASSWARE	GARNISH
2000s	Vermouth cocktail	Stirred	Coupe glass	Cucumber slice

COBBLE HILL

The Cobble Hill is a creation from the early days of Milk & Honey, when the members of the team were frequently using cucumber in their cocktails. Sasha Petraske, founder of Milk & Honey, and Sam Ross combined Amaro Montenegro, dry vermouth, and cucumber resulting in a light and floral take on a classic **Manhattan** (page 80).

2 thin **cucumber slices**

2 oz (60ml) **rye whiskey**

½ oz (15ml) **Amaro Montenegro**

½ oz (15ml) **dry vermouth**

1 In a mixing glass, gently muddle the cucumber.

2 Add the remaining ingredients and ice. Stir for 15 to 30 seconds.

3 Double strain into a chilled coupe glass.

4 Garnish with a slice of cucumber.

Don't overwork the cucumber. A light muddle is more than enough to impart the flavours into the drink.

ORIGINATED	TYPE	METHOD	GLASSWARE	GARNISH
1970s	Miscellaneous	Built	Old-fashioned glass	Lemon twist

GODFATHER

No one has claimed to be the creator of the Godfather, but the amaretto brand Disaronno has certainly taken advantage of the popularity of the 1970s cocktail. The recipe originally called for equal parts Scotch whisky and amaretto, although this results in a very sweet drink. Most modern tastes prefer a smaller proportion of amaretto, resulting in a drier and more subtle almond flavour.

2 oz (60ml) blended **Scotch whisky**

¼–½ oz (7.5–15ml) **amaretto**

1 Measure ingredients over a large ice cube into an old-fashioned glass.

2 Stir until chilled.

3 Garnish with a twist of lemon.

Try splitting the amaretto with an Islay whisky for something a little more smoky.

ORIGINATED	TYPE	METHOD	GLASSWARE	GARNISH
Circa 2000	Sour	Shaken	Old-fashioned glass	Lemon peel

GOLD RUSH

Sasha Petraske opened Milk & Honey in 1999, and the Gold Rush was one of the first truly successful creations from the bar. Surprisingly, it wasn't created by Sasha or anyone on his team. It was created by his longtime friend, T.J. Siegal, whilst he was sitting at the Milk & Honey bar enjoying a Bourbon Sour after a long shift in Midtown.

Petraske told him about a honey syrup he was concocting, and Siegal requested another sour made using the syrup. Sasha used a common sour format of 2 ounces (60ml) spirit, ¾ ounce (22.5ml) juice, and ¾ ounce (22.5ml) sweetener, and it was an instant hit. Over the course of the next 12 years, Sasha featured the drink at several of his prominent bars.

Jim Meehan tried the Gold Rush on his first visit to Milk & Honey in 2003. The drink had a big impact on Meehan, who stated that it fundamentally changed the way he viewed cocktails. He went on to make it at every bar he worked at and later included the recipe in *The PDT Cocktail Book*, helping to grow its popularity.

2 oz (60ml) **bourbon whiskey**

¾ oz (22.5ml) **honey syrup** (page 29)

¾ oz (22.5ml) freshly squeezed **lemon juice**

1 In a cocktail shaker, combine all ingredients.

2 Add ice and shake for 10 to 12 seconds.

3 Strain over fresh ice into an old-fashioned glass.

4 Garnish with a lemon peel.

Try multiple honey ratios to find your sweet spot! The higher honey-to-water ratios result in a more intense honey flavour and a silky texture.

ORIGINATED	TYPE	METHOD	GLASSWARE	GARNISH
2005	Vermouth cocktail	Stirred	Coupe glass	Lemon twist

GREENPOINT

The Greenpoint was created by Michael McIlroy at the legendary Milk & Honey bar in 2005. The eponymous cocktail follows suit with the likes of the **Red Hook** (page 96); a neighbourhood namesake cocktail inspired by the **Manhattan** (page 80) and the **Brooklyn** (page 63).

2 oz (60ml) **rye whiskey**

1 oz (30ml) **Punt e Mes vermouth**

1 tsp (5ml) **Yellow Chartreuse**

1 dash of **Angostura bitters**

1   In a mixing glass, combine all ingredients.

2   Add ice and stir for 15 to 30 seconds.

3   Strain into a chilled coupe glass.

4   Garnish with a lemon twist.

There are countless subtle variations on the Greenpoint. Try using your preferred sweet vermouth to compare, or perhaps increase the Yellow Chartreuse for more honeyed, herbal notes.

ORIGINATED	TYPE	METHOD	GLASSWARE	GARNISH
1876	Old-fashioned	Stirred	Old-fashioned glass	Lemon twist

IMPROVED WHISKEY COCKTAIL

"Improved" cocktails are simple variations on spirit-forward classics and often include the addition of orange Curaçao, maraschino liqueur, or absinthe. The Improved Whiskey Cocktail is an Old Fashioned with the addition of a small measure of maraschino liqueur and an absinthe rinse.

This recipe is a perfect example of how subtle changes to a cocktail can have a profound effect on a drink's flavour profile. The dash of absinthe brings an underlying note of anise, whilst the maraschino adds a sweet nuttiness.

2 oz (60ml) **rye whiskey**

¼ oz (7.5ml) **maraschino liqueur**

¼ oz (7.5ml) **simple syrup** (page 28)

2 dashes of **Angostura bitters**

1 dash of **absinthe,** to rinse the glass

1 In a mixing glass, combine the rye whiskey, maraschino liqueur, simple syrup, and bitters.

2 Add ice and stir for 15 to 30 seconds.

3 To a chilled old-fashioned glass, add a dash of absinthe. Gently rotate the glass on an angle to coat the inside.

4 Strain over a large ice cube into the prepared glass.

5 Garnish with a lemon twist.

Why not try experimenting with your own improved cocktail? Try changing the base spirit, liqueur, and/or bitters combination.

ORIGINATED	TYPE	METHOD	GLASSWARE	GARNISH
2013	Sour	Shaken	Old-fashioned glass	Cucumber, mint sprig

IRISH MAID

Jack McGarry from The Dead Rabbit in New York City created this variation on Sam Ross' modern classic, the London Maid (a.k.a. Old Maid), and this is my favourite of the two. Whilst there are a considerable number of changes, it maintains the template of the Maid category of drinks— spirit/citrus/sweetener/cucumber.

The original London Maid consists of gin, lime, simple syrup, cucumber, and mint (no elderflower liqueur). Other noteworthy variations include: the Kentucky Maid (bourbon whiskey), the Polish Maid (vodka), and the Mexican Maid (tequila). Discover your favourite Maid by comparing them all.

3 **cucumber slices**

2 oz (60ml) **Irish whiskey**

½ oz (15ml) **St-Germain Elderflower liqueur**

¾ oz (22.5ml) freshly squeezed **lemon juice**

¾ oz (22.5ml) **simple syrup** (page 28)

1   In a cocktail shaker, gently muddle the cucumber.

2   Add the remaining ingredients and ice. Shake for 10 to 12 seconds.

3   Double strain over fresh ice into an old-fashioned glass.

4   Garnish with a cucumber wheel and mint sprig.

ORIGINATED	TYPE	METHOD	GLASSWARE	GARNISH
2005	Vermouth cocktail	Stirred	Coupe glass	Maraschino cherry

LITTLE ITALY

The Little Italy is an exceptional variation on a Manhattan created by Audrey Saunders in 2005 at the iconic Pegu Club in New York. It's a tribute to the Little Italy neighbourhood, which bordered the bar, as well as a nod to the combination of Italian and American ingredients in the drink.

Audrey has numerous other cocktail claims to fame including the **Gin Gin Mule** (page 147) and the **Earl Grey MarTEAni** (page 132). She has joined the ranks of Ada Coleman and Julie Reiner as one of the most accomplished and respected female bartenders in the modern cocktail era. Her dedication to the craft can be witnessed throughout her journey, starting with her role as Dale DeGroff's apprentice and culminating in the opening of the Pegu Club, where she launched a gin-centric menu in a cocktail scene that was dominated by vodka drinks.

2 oz (60ml) **rye whiskey**

¾ oz (22.5ml) **sweet vermouth**

½ oz (15ml) **Cynar**

1   In a mixing glass, combine all ingredients.

2   Add ice and stir for 15 to 30 seconds.

3   Strain into a chilled coupe glass.

4   Garnish with a skewered maraschino cherry.

If you want to keep it true to the original, use Rittenhouse rye and Martini & Rossi Rosso vermouth.

ORIGINATED	TYPE	METHOD	GLASSWARE	GARNISH
Circa 1882	Vermouth cocktail	Stirred	Coupe glass	Maraschino cherry

MANHATTAN

The original Manhattan, created at the Manhattan Club, was an equal parts affair of whiskey and sweet vermouth with a touch of gum syrup and a dash or two of bitters. This would clearly make for a far sweeter version compared to the 2:1 whiskey-to-vermouth ratio commonly used today.

The first Italian vermouth hit the shores in the United States in 1838, but it wasn't until 1884 that vermouth started appearing in cocktail books, helping it to flourish.

2 oz (60ml) **bourbon** or **rye whiskey**

1 oz (30ml) **sweet vermouth**

2 dashes of **Angostura bitters**

1 In a mixing glass, combine all ingredients.

2 Add ice and stir for 15 to 30 seconds.

3 Strain into a chilled coupe glass.

4 Garnish with a skewered maraschino cherry.

Orange bitters are an excellent alternative to aromatic bitters.

A dash of absinthe makes a unique addition to the drink.

ORIGINATED	TYPE	METHOD	GLASSWARE	GARNISH
Circa 2011	Sour	Shaken	Old-fashioned glass	Mint sprig

MIDNIGHT STINGER

The original Stinger is a pre-Prohibition cocktail composed of cognac and white crème de menthe in a 2:1 ratio. This is a modern take by Sam Ross.

Sam Ross was a bartender at Milk & Honey and is now co-owner of Attaboy. He's created a long list of modern cocktails, including the **Paper Plane** (page 92) and **Penicillin** (page 95). The team at Attaboy forgo the usual menu and rely on their "bartender's choice" format. The Midnight Stinger is Sam's go-to for whiskey/citrus/bitter.

1 oz (30ml) **bourbon whiskey**

1 oz (30ml) **Fernet Branca**

¾ oz (22.5ml) freshly squeezed **lemon juice**

¾ oz (22.5ml) **simple syrup** (page 28)

1   In a cocktail shaker, combine all ingredients.

2   Add ice and shake for 10 to 12 seconds.

3   Strain over pebble ice into an old-fashioned glass.

4   Garnish with a mint sprig.

Whilst this is a great drink to introduce one to Fernet, it can be bracingly bitter. Try substituting an alternative amaro if the Fernet is not to your taste.

ORIGINATED	TYPE	METHOD	GLASSWARE	GARNISH
1803	Julep	Built	Julep cup or old-fashioned glass	Mint sprig

MINT JULEP

The earliest versions of Juleps from the 1770s were a combination of rum (or French brandy), sugar, and water but it's the modern Mint Julep, made with bourbon whiskey, that has become ubiquitous. A phylloxera epidemic in the mid-1800s wiped out many French vineyards, which restricted the French brandy supply and cemented whiskey as the spirit of choice for the Julep.

The Mint Julep became the official drink of the Kentucky Derby in 1938 and has remained synonymous with the event ever since.

8 **mint leaves**

½ oz (15ml) **simple syrup** (page 28)

2½ oz (75ml) **bourbon whiskey**

1 In a julep cup (or old-fashioned glass), muddle the mint with the simple syrup.

2 Add the bourbon and fill the glass with pebble ice.

3 Swizzle until the exterior of the cup is frosty.

4 Top with more pebble ice and garnish with a large mint sprig.

Try a Peach Julep if you can secure a bottle of peach brandy.

ORIGINATED	TYPE	METHOD	GLASSWARE	GARNISH
1883	Sour	Shaken	Old-fashioned glass	None

NEW YORK SOUR

The **Whiskey Sour** (page 115) was first published in Jerry Thomas' *The Bartender's Guide* in 1862, but it was a few decades before a Chicago bartender added a red wine float to the drink. The sour with the addition of "'claret" went by several names: the Continental Sour, the Southern Whiskey Sour, and later, the New York Sour—the name which was settled on after Prohibition. A dry red wine such as a Malbec or Syrah is preferred.

2 oz (60ml) **bourbon** or **rye whiskey**

¾ oz (22.5ml) freshly squeezed **lemon juice**

¾ oz (22.5ml) **simple syrup** (page 28)

1 oz (30ml) **red wine** (Malbec or Syrah recommended)

1   In a cocktail shaker, combine the whiskey, lemon juice, and simple syrup.

2   Add ice and shake for 10 to 12 seconds.

3   Strain over fresh ice into an old-fashioned glass.

4   Gently pour the red wine on top to create a layered effect.

If you like a Whiskey Sour with egg white, feel free to add it to your New York Sour as well.

ORIGINATED	TYPE	METHOD	GLASSWARE	GARNISH
1880	Cocktail	Stirred	Old-fashioned glass	Orange twist

OLD FASHIONED

The term "cocktail" was defined in 1806 and referred to a drink consisting of spirit, water, sugar, and bitters. During the late 1800s, it was common for bartenders to use whiskey, brandy, or Dutch gin (genever) when a cocktail was ordered. Bartenders were also making "improved" versions, which often included orange curaçao, maraschino liqueur, or absinthe.

At the time, drinkers had no idea what to expect from one bar to the next, so people started requesting an "old-fashioned whiskey cocktail" to ensure they received a cocktail made with whiskey without any additions. By 1880, this expression was shortened to simply become an "Old Fashioned."

1 **sugar cube**

1 tsp **water**

2 dashes of **Angostura bitters**

2 oz (60ml) **bourbon** or **rye whiskey**

1   In a mixing glass, combine the sugar, water, and bitters.

2   Muddle the sugar and then add the whiskey.

3   Add ice and stir for 15 to 30 seconds.

4   Strain over a large ice cube into an old-fashioned glass.

5   Garnish with an orange twist.

Garnish with a twist of lemon, orange, or both—it's completely up to you.

ORIGINATED	TYPE	METHOD	GLASSWARE	GARNISH
Circa 1922	Vermouth cocktail	Stirred	Coupe glass	Lemon twist

OLD PAL

The Old Pal is a close relative of the **Negroni** (page 160) and **Boulevardier** (page 60). The key difference, compared to its cousins, is the use of dry vermouth. The recipe was first printed in Harry McElhone's *ABC of Mixing Cocktails* but is credited to William Robinson, a sports editor in Paris at the time who often referred to his acquaintances as "old pals."

The classic ratio is equal parts, but many modern tastes will prefer a 2:1:1 ratio in favour of the whiskey.

1½ oz (45ml) **rye whiskey**
¾ oz (22.5ml) **Campari**
¾ oz (22.5ml) **dry vermouth**

1 In a mixing glass, combine all ingredients.

2 Add ice and stir for 15 to 30 seconds.

3 Strain into a chilled coupe glass.

4 Garnish with a lemon twist.

If you want to stay true to the original, use a Canadian whisky.

ORIGINATED	TYPE	METHOD	GLASSWARE	GARNISH
2007	Sour	Shaken	Coupe glass	Mini paper plane

PAPER PLANE

The Paper Plane is a beautifully balanced creation with four equal-part ingredients that come together to produce another vibrant cocktail by Australian-born bartender Sam Ross.

Sam's former Milk & Honey colleague, Toby Maloney, asked him to help with an original cocktail for the opening menu of the Violet Hour in Chicago. His recipe originally called for Campari, but a few days after sending the recipe to Toby, he tweaked the recipe by using Aperol in its place, which went on to become a mainstay.

¾ oz (22.5ml) **bourbon whiskey**

¾ oz (22.5ml) **Aperol**

¾ oz (22.5ml) **Amaro Nonino**

¾ oz (22.5ml) freshly squeezed **lemon juice**

1   In a cocktail shaker, combine all ingredients.

2   Add ice and shake for 10 to 12 seconds.

3   Double strain into a coupe glass.

4   Garnish with a mini paper airplane, if desired.

I recommend trying the first iteration of the recipe that included Campari—although the use of Aperol does bring the Amaro Nonino to the forefront.

Amaro Montenegro is the best substitute for Amaro Nonino, if you cannot acquire a bottle.

ORIGINATED	TYPE	METHOD	GLASSWARE	GARNISH
2005	Sour	Shaken	Old-fashioned glass	Candied ginger

PENICILLIN

The Penicillin is another ingenious creation by Australian bartender Sam Ross. It was created during his time at Milk & Honey in New York and is a riff on another Milk & Honey drink, the **Gold Rush** (page 71).

Sam introduced countless bartenders to the Penicillin during his time as a bar consultant. They helped spread the drink, increasing its popularity and making it one of the most well-known and riffed-on modern classics.

The Medicina Latina is one of those many riffs on the Penicillin. Sasha Petraske brings it closer to Margarita territory by using blanco tequila instead of Scotch whisky, a smoky mezcal float instead of Islay whisky, and lime juice instead of lemon.

2 oz (60ml) blended **Scotch whisky** (Famous Grouse recommended)

¾ oz (22.5ml) freshly squeezed **lemon juice**

⅓ oz (10ml) **honey syrup** (page 29)

⅓ oz (10ml) **ginger syrup** (page 29)

¼ oz (7.5ml) **Islay whisky**

1   In a cocktail shaker, combine all ingredients except the Islay whisky.

2   Add ice and shake for 10 to 12 seconds.

3   Strain over fresh ice into an old-fashioned glass.

4   Float the Islay whisky on top (or use an atomiser to spray atop the drink).

5   Garnish with a piece of candied ginger.

Instead of ginger syrup, muddle fresh ginger with simple syrup.

Sam originally used the super-smoky Compass Box The Peat Monster Scotch whisky for the float.

ORIGINATED	TYPE	METHOD	GLASSWARE	GARNISH
2003	Vermouth cocktail	Stirred	Coupe glass	None

RED HOOK

The Red Hook is a Manhattan-Brooklyn mash-up created by Italian bartender Vincenzo "Enzo" Errico, who was trained by legendary British bartender Dick Bradsell, creator of the **Espresso Martini** (page 284). Vincenzo was poached by Sasha Petraske and worked behind the bar at Milk & Honey in New York for several years. He created several modern classics whilst at Milk & Honey, including the Red Hook and the **Enzoni** (page 136).

Vincenzo's Red Hook was a revelation for New York bartenders, and it inspired many other cocktails named after neighbourhoods including the **Greenpoint** (page 72), the **Bensonhurst** (page 55) and the **Little Italy** (page 79).

2 oz (60ml) **rye whiskey**

½ oz (15ml) **maraschino liqueur** (Luxardo recommended)

½ oz (15ml) **Punt e Mes vermouth**

1   In a mixing glass, combine all ingredients.

2   Add ice and stir for 15 to 30 seconds.

3   Strain into a chilled coupe glass.

Luxardo maraschino liqueur has been around for over 200 years. It's the go-to maraschino liqueur.

ORIGINATED	TYPE	METHOD	GLASSWARE	GARNISH
Circa 1939	Vermouth cocktail	Stirred	Stemmed cocktail glass	Lemon twist

REMEMBER THE MAINE

Remember the Maine was featured in *The Gentleman's Companion* by Charles H. Baker, which was published in 1939. The name references a popular slogan from 1898, when a mysterious explosion destroyed the USS Maine in Havana, Cuba. The Spanish were blamed for the tragic demise of the battleship and "Remember the Maine! To hell with Spain!" became a rallying cry for action that culminated in the Spanish-American war.

This sweeter style, spirit-forward drink is a cross between the **Manhattan** (page 80) and the **Sazerac** (page 107).

2 oz (60ml) **rye whiskey**

¾ oz (22.5ml) **sweet vermouth**

⅓ oz (10ml) **Heering cherry liqueur**

1 dash of **absinthe**

1   In a mixing glass, combine all ingredients.

2   Add ice and stir for 15 to 30 seconds.

3   Strain into a chilled stemmed cocktail glass.

4   Garnish with a lemon twist (or maraschino cherry).

Don't forget to always store your vermouth in the fridge!

ORIGINATED	TYPE	METHOD	GLASSWARE	GARNISH
2004	Cocktail	Stirred	Coupe glass	Flamed orange zest

REVOLVER

San Francisco bartender Jon Santer created this coffee-laced riff on a Manhattan after he was tasked with moving a case of rye-heavy Bulleit bourbon. His inspiration came from a friend who would often add crème de cacao to his Manhattans.

Jon tried adding rum-based Tia Maria coffee liqueur to his own Manhattan and finished it with a few dashes of orange bitters and a flamed orange zest. He took the drink with him to Bourbon & Branch in 2006. A year later, it was featured in the *Wall Street Journal* and was subsequently picked up by the Milk & Honey family of bars, which cemented the Revolver as a modern classic.

2 oz (60ml) **bourbon whiskey** (Bulleit originally)

½ oz (15ml) **coffee liqueur** (Tia Maria originally)

2 dashes of **orange bitters**

1   In a mixing glass, combine all ingredients.

2   Add ice and stir for 15 to 30 seconds.

3   Strain into a chilled coupe glass.

4   Garnish with a flamed orange zest.

Choose your favourite coffee liqueur. I prefer using Mr Black Cold Brew coffee liqueur, although you may want to add a touch of simple syrup to sweeten the drink.

ORIGINATED	TYPE	METHOD	GLASSWARE	GARNISH
Circa 1894	Vermouth cocktail	Stirred	Coupe glass	Maraschino cherry

ROB ROY

The Rob Roy emerged only a short number of years after the creation of the **Manhattan** (page 80). It's only a small step from a classic Manhattan, yet it results in a far different cocktail.

According to *The Waldorf Astoria Bar Book* by Frank Caiafa, the drink was inspired by the opera show *Rob Roy*. The show was based around a Scottish Robin Hood-like hero named Rob Roy MacGregor.

2 oz (60ml) **blended Scotch whisky**

1 oz (30ml) **sweet vermouth**

2 dashes of **orange bitters**

1   In a mixing glass, combine all ingredients.

2   Add ice and stir for 15 to 30 seconds.

3   Strain into a chilled coupe glass.

4   Garnish with a maraschino cherry.

Opt for ¾ ounce sweet vermouth if you prefer a drier drink.

Adding Benedictine to a Rob Roy results in a Bobby Burns.

ORIGINATED	TYPE	METHOD	GLASSWARE	GARNISH
1937	Miscellaneous	Stirred	Old-fashioned glass	None

RUSTY NAIL

The recipe for Drambuie, an aged Scotch whisky liqueur flavoured with herbs and spices and sweetened with honey, dates back to at least 1746. It is a sweet liqueur, so fortifying it with a blended Scotch whisky tames the sweetness and brings subtlety to the herbal notes.

2 oz (60ml) blended **Scotch whisky**

½ oz (15ml) **Drambuie**

1   In a mixing glass, combine all ingredients.

2   Add ice and stir for 15 to 30 seconds.

3   Strain over a large ice cube into an old-fashioned glass.

Garnish with a lemon or orange twist, if desired.

ORIGINATED	TYPE	METHOD	GLASSWARE	GARNISH
1899	Cocktail	Stirred	Old-fashioned glass	None

SAZERAC

The Sazerac cocktail emerged from the Sazerac Coffee House in New Orleans whilst the bar owner was the local agent for Sazerac de Forge et Fils Cognac. It's not a far stretch to say that cognac could have been the original base spirit, yet several cocktail historians believe it was most likely a rye whiskey cocktail from the very beginning.

Rye whiskey is my preferred choice, but cognac (or a combination of cognac and rye whiskey) also makes a fine Sazerac. Using a combination of Angostura and Peychaud's bitters is also popular, but the Peychaud's is integral.

1 **sugar cube** or 1 tsp **sugar**

2–5 dashes of **Peychaud's bitters**

2 oz (60ml) **rye whiskey**

1 dash of **absinthe,** to rinse the glass

Lemon peel

1   Add the sugar to a mixing glass and soak with bitters.

2   Muddle the sugar and then add the whiskey.

3   Add ice and stir for 15 to 30 seconds.

4   To a chilled old-fashioned glass, add a dash of absinthe. Gently rotate the glass on an angle to coat the inside.

5   Strain the drink into the prepared glass.

6   Express lemon oils over the drink and discard the peel.

Rye whiskey, cognac, or a combination of both—each make an excellent Sazerac.

Don't hold back on the Peychaud's bitters.

ORIGINATED	TYPE	METHOD	GLASSWARE	GARNISH
2008	Sour	Shaken	Coupe glass	None

TRINIDAD SOUR

Giuseppe González created the Trinidad Sour for Star Chefs, an online platform that supports the hospitality industry. Whilst he was working at Clover Club in Brooklyn, he presented the drink to the owner Julie Reiner. She shut down the idea of putting it on the menu, as she thought no one would order the bitters-heavy drink and it was far too expensive. When Julie went on a consulting trip, Giuseppe sneakily reprinted the bar menus to include his cocktail. A fellow bartender from a nearby Brooklyn bar, Drink, tried it and started serving it at his bar, where it took off. Giuseppe moved on to another New York bar, Dutch Kills, and further spread the cocktail.

1½ oz (45ml) **Angostura bitters**

½ oz (15ml) **rye whiskey**

1 oz (30ml) **orgeat** (page 30)

¾ oz (22.5ml) freshly squeezed **lemon juice**

1 In a cocktail shaker, combine all ingredients.

2 Add ice and shake for 10 to 12 seconds.

3 Double strain into a chilled coupe glass.

You'll need a bigger bottle of Angostura bitters if you add this to your rotation.

ORIGINATED	TYPE	METHOD	GLASSWARE	GARNISH
Circa 1903	Sour	Shaken	Coupe glass	None

WARD 8

Grenadine was in vogue at the start of the twentieth century, and it was the Ward 8 that kicked off a number of classic cocktails featuring this ingredient. These cocktails include the Jack Rose, the Pink Lady, the Mexican Firing Squad, and the El Presidente.

There are a number of Ward 8 recipes, but this version features my preferred ratio and is also how the drink is served at Ward Eight bar in Chicago. One welcome addition that they do not employ is a sprig of fresh mint, which is well worth trying for comparison.

2 oz (60ml) **rye whiskey**

½ oz (15ml) freshly squeezed **lemon juice**

½ oz (15ml) freshly squeezed **orange juice**

½ oz (15ml) **grenadine** (page 30)

1   In a cocktail shaker, combine all ingredients.

2   Add ice and shake for 10 to 12 seconds.

3   Double strain into a chilled coupe glass.

Add a sprig of fresh mint to your tin before shaking. You'll thank me later.

ORIGINATED	TYPE	METHOD	GLASSWARE	GARNISH
1830s	Smash	Shaken	Old-fashioned glass	Lemon, mint sprig

WHISKEY SMASH

Originally, the Smash family of cocktails was only a step away from the Julep family, with the main difference being additional garnishes. Modern versions of the Smash have evolved significantly and often contain citrus in the form of muddled lemon or lemon juice and herbs such as mint or basil. Today, a Smash is more reminiscent of a **Whiskey Sour** (page 115) than a Julep.

This modern version of the Whiskey Smash was created by Dale DeGroff.

3–4 **mint leaves**

½ **lemon,** cut into quarters

2 oz (60ml) **bourbon whiskey**

¾ oz (22.5ml) **simple syrup** (page 28)

1 Place the mint and lemon wedges in a cocktail shaker (add the mint first) and muddle briefly. (Don't over muddle the mint.)

2 Add the whiskey and simple syrup.

3 Add ice and shake for 10 to 12 seconds.

4 Double strain over fresh ice into an old-fashioned glass.

5 Garnish with a lemon wedge and sprig of mint.

You can use 1 ounce (30ml) freshly squeezed lemon juice instead of muddled lemons if you prefer, but I recommend using a citrus press, which will replicate the extraction of lemon oil from the skin.

ORIGINATED	TYPE	METHOD	GLASSWARE	GARNISH
1858	Sour	Shaken	Old-fashioned glass	Maraschino cherry, orange slice

WHISKEY SOUR

The Whiskey Sour was created in the mid-1800s and has stood the test of time. There were a few tweaks in its early stages, but otherwise not much has changed for more than 150 years. *Haney's Stewards & Barkeeper's Manual,* published in 1869, featured a recipe that closely resembles a modern version of the Whiskey Sour. This recipe was a stirred drink (as opposed to shaken) and contained slightly less lemon juice, resulting in a sweeter drink.

The Whiskey Sour is often made with an egg white for added texture, although this addition was not part of the original recipe. When made with egg white, the drink is known as a Boston Sour.

2 oz (60ml) **bourbon** or **rye whiskey**

¾ oz (22.5ml) freshly squeezed **lemon juice**

¾ oz (22.5ml) **simple syrup** (page 28)

½ oz (15ml) **egg white** (optional)

1 spray (or dash) of **Angostura bitters**

1   In a cocktail shaker, combine all ingredients.

2   If using egg white, dry shake (without ice) for 5 to 10 seconds. Then add ice and shake for 10 to 12 seconds.

3   Strain over fresh ice into an old-fashioned glass.

4   Garnish with a skewered maraschino and orange slice.

Use the whiskey sour as a template and customise it to your liking. Bourbon or rye whiskey? Egg white or not? Over ice or up? It's your choice.

ORIGINATED	TYPE	METHOD	GLASSWARE	GARNISH
Circa 1937	Sour	Shaken	Coupe glass	Lemon twist

20TH CENTURY

The 20th Century cocktail was created as homage to the high-end passenger rail that operated between Chicago and New York for 65 years. It was first featured in the 1937 *Cafe Royal Cocktail Book*. The unlikely trio of gin, lemon, and chocolate works surprisingly well, and the format of the drink is similar to the **Corpse Reviver No. 2** (page 128).

1½ oz (45ml) **gin**

¾ oz (22.5ml) **Lillet Blanc**

¾ oz (22.5ml) **white crème de cacao**

¾ oz (22.5ml) freshly squeezed **lemon juice**

1 In a cocktail shaker, combine all ingredients.

2 Add ice and shake for 10 to 12 seconds.

3 Double strain into a coupe glass.

4 Garnish with a lemon twist.

Ensure you use white crème de cacao. If you use brown crème de cacao, the drink won't look appealing.

ORIGINATED	TYPE	METHOD	GLASSWARE	GARNISH
2008	Smash	Shaken	Old-fashioned glass	Basil sprig

BASIL SMASH

Joerg Meyer, the owner of the Le Lion bar in Germany, was inspired to create the Basil Smash after a trip to New York. Whilst on his travels, he sampled Dale DeGroff's Whiskey Smash at the Pegu Club. He was instantly hooked and quickly returned to Hamburg to begin experimenting.

His creation debuted on the drinks menu as the Gin Pesto but the name was later changed to the Gin Basil Smash. For his choice of gin, Joerg moved from Tanqueray to Beefeater before eventually settling on Rutte Celery Gin, as savoury gins work best for this drink.

Joerg and his team have made three to five hundred Basil Smashes every week since 2008, making him one of the biggest sellers of Rutte gin.

10 **basil leaves**

2 oz (60 ml) **gin** (Rutte Celery recommended)

1 oz (30 ml) freshly squeezed **lemon juice**

¾ oz (22.5 ml) **simple syrup** (page 28)

1 In a cocktail shaker, gently muddle the basil leaves.

2 Add the gin, lemon juice, and simple syrup.

3 Add ice and shake for 10 to 12 seconds.

4 Double strain over fresh ice into an old-fashioned glass.

5 Garnish with a sprig of basil.

Try making a Basil Smash with different styles of gin to find your favourite.

ORIGINATED	TYPE	METHOD	GLASSWARE	GARNISH
1920s	Sour	Shaken	Coupe glass	None

BEES KNEES

The Bees Knees is a simple variant on the classic Gin Sour utilising honey in place of sugar as the sweetener. The drink was created by Frank Meier, the first head bartender of the Hôtel Ritz Paris, during the 1920s. The Bees Knees features sweet honey and highlights the botanical notes of your preferred gin.

2 oz (60ml) **gin**

1 oz (30ml) freshly squeezed **lemon juice**

¾ oz (22.5ml) **honey syrup** (page 29)

1　In a cocktail shaker, combine all ingredients.

2　Add ice and shake for 10 to 12 seconds.

3　Double strain into a chilled coupe glass.

A London dry gin will add more typical juniper notes, whilst a contemporary gin with citrus and/or floral notes will highlight the lemon and honey.

Want to try a different spirit? Using bourbon whiskey creates a **Gold Rush** *(page 71), a light Cuban rum creates a Honeysuckle, and Jamaican rum creates a Honey Bee.*

ORIGINATED	TYPE	METHOD	GLASSWARE	GARNISH
1984	Sour	Shaken	Old-fashioned glass	Blackberries, lemon slice

BRAMBLE

The Bramble is a delicious creation by legendary bartender Dick Bradsell, who also developed the cult favourite **Espresso Martini** (page 284). Dick created the Bramble as a sentimental play on a **Singapore Sling** (page 171) but with a nostalgic nod to flavours of his childhood in Britain—namely, blackberries. Crushed ice is a key component to the drink, providing dilution as well as helping to provide a cascading effect when adding the crème de mûre.

2 oz (60ml) **gin**

¾ oz (22.5ml) freshly squeezed **lemon juice**

¼ oz (7.5ml) **simple syrup** (page 28)

½ oz (15ml) **crème de mûre**

1　In a cocktail shaker, combine all ingredients except the crème de mûre.

2　Add ice and shake for 10 to 12 seconds.

3　Strain over pebble ice into an old-fashioned glass and pour the crème de mûre on top.

4　Garnish with a blackberry and a lemon slice.

Blackberries are seasonal, so feel free to omit the berry garnish if fresh fruit is not available.

ORIGINATED	TYPE	METHOD	GLASSWARE	GARNISH
Circa 1920	Sour	Shaken	Coupe glass	None

CHARLIE CHAPLIN

The Charlie Chaplin was created at New York City's Waldorf Astoria hotel prior to the 1920s. It was featured in the 1934 *Old Waldorf Astoria Bar Book* but a later revision altered the proportions. Due to the differing sugar content of apricot liqueurs and sloe gins, you may need to tweak the ratios to maintain balance.

1 oz (30ml) **sloe gin**

1 oz (30ml) **apricot brandy liqueur**

1 oz (30ml) freshly squeezed **lime juice**

1   In a cocktail shaker, combine all ingredients.

2   Add ice and shake for 10 to 12 seconds.

3   Double strain into a chilled coupe glass.

Try replacing the sloe gin with an alternate fruit-flavoured gin.

ORIGINATED	TYPE	METHOD	GLASSWARE	GARNISH
1901	Sour	Shaken	Coupe glass	Raspberries

CLOVER CLUB

The Clover Club was created in 1901, during an era when there were countless "gentlemen's clubs" that celebrated themselves with eponymous signature cocktails, such as the Pendennis Club, the Royal Bermuda Yacht Club, and the Pegu Club. The original creator is unknown but Michael Killackey, head bartender at the Waldorf Astoria, first noted the recipe and was partially responsible for spreading the drink's popularity.

The Clover Club was named after a men's club that congregated at Philadelphia's Bellevue-Stratford Hotel. The manager of the hotel later moved to the Waldorf Astoria along with the drink.

In 1909, Paul Lowe featured the recipe with the inclusion of dry vermouth in *How to Mix and Serve*. The vermouth is a great addition to the classic Clover Club, although it is omitted in most written recipes. It was Paul's recipe that was resurrected on Julie Reiner's drinks menu circa 2007 at her Brooklyn bar, Clover Club.

1½ oz (45ml) **London dry gin**

½ oz (15ml) **dry vermouth**

½ oz (15ml) freshly squeezed **lemon juice**

½ oz (15ml) **raspberry syrup** (page 29)

½ oz (15ml) **egg white**

1 In a cocktail shaker, combine all ingredients.

2 Dry shake (without ice) for 5 to 10 seconds.

3 Add ice and shake for 10 to 12 seconds.

4 Double strain into a chilled coupe glass.

5 Garnish with skewered raspberries, if desired.

Don't want to prepare a large batch of raspberry syrup? Replace the raspberry syrup with simple syrup and muddle 3 fresh raspberries before shaking the cocktail.

ORIGINATED	TYPE	METHOD	GLASSWARE	GARNISH
1930	Sour	Shaken	Coupe glass	Lemon twist

CORPSE REVIVER NO. 2

The Corpse Reviver category of cocktails can be traced back to the 1870s, but it wasn't until Harry Craddock's 1930 *The Savoy Cocktail Book* that the No. 2 received a mention. Corpse Revivers were a category of cocktails known for their apparent ability to relieve a hangover. No. 1 and No. 2 are the longstanding creations of the category, although the Corpse Reviver No. 2 is a clear favourite for the majority of people.

The recipe originally called for Kina Lillet, which has long been unavailable, so two recommended substitutes are Cocchi Americano or Lillet Blanc.

¾ oz (22.5ml) **London dry gin**

¾ oz (22.5ml) **Cointreau**

¾ oz (22.5ml) **Lillet Blanc**

¾ oz (22.5ml) freshly squeezed **lemon juice**

1 dash of **absinthe**, to rinse glass

1 In a cocktail shaker, combine all ingredients except absinthe.

2 Add ice and shake for 10 to 12 seconds.

3 Rinse a chilled coupe glass with absinthe.

4 Double strain into the prepared glass and garnish with a lemon twist, if desired.

Stick with the Corpse Reviver No. 2—it's by far the best of the Corpse Reviver iterations.

ORIGINATED	TYPE	METHOD	GLASSWARE	GARNISH
2000s	Sour	Shaken	Coupe glass	None

COSMONAUT

The Cosmonaut was created by industry legend Sasha Petraske, one of the founders of the historic New York establishment Milk & Honey. It's a simple three-ingredient variation on a Breakfast Martini and named as a cheeky retort to the **Cosmopolitan** (page 280).

My favourite yet relatively unknown creation of Sasha's is the **Dominicana** (page 203).

2 oz (60ml) **gin**

¾ oz (22.5ml) freshly squeezed **lemon juice**

1 tsp **raspberry jam,** heaped

1   In a cocktail shaker, combine all ingredients.

2   Add ice and shake for 10 to 12 seconds.

3   Double strain into a chilled coupe glass or other stemmed cocktail glass.

No raspberry jam on hand? Try substituting in another jam! Blueberry? Apricot?

ORIGINATED	TYPE	METHOD	GLASSWARE	GARNISH
Early 2000s	Sour	Shaken	Coupe glass	Lemon twist

EARL GREY MAR-TEA-NI

The Earl Grey MarTEAni is a simple and unique variation on a classic Gin Sour. It was created in the early 2000s by Audrey Saunders of New York's well-respected Pegu Club. The tea adds notes of bergamot and soft tannins that complement the gin's botanicals. Audrey prefers Tanqueray gin.

1½ oz (45ml) **Earl Grey-infused London dry gin** (see note)

1 oz (30ml) **simple syrup** (page 28)

¾ oz (22.5ml) freshly squeezed **lemon juice**

1 **egg white**

1   In a cocktail shaker, combine all ingredients.

2   Dry shake (without ice) for 5 to 10 seconds.

3   Add ice and shake for 10 to 12 seconds.

4   Double strain into a chilled coupe glass.

5   Garnish with a twist of lemon.

To make infused gin, add 2 tablespoons loose Earl Grey tea to 375ml gin and steep for 2 to 4 hours. Strain with a cheesecloth and rebottle.

ORIGINATED	TYPE	METHOD	GLASSWARE	GARNISH
2004	Sour	Shaken	Coupe glass	Cucumber, mint sprig

EASTSIDE

The Eastside cocktail is a subtle variation on the Southside. The muddled cucumber makes a welcome addition to the citrus and mint flavour combination.

George Delgado first created his Southside variation at Libation in New York City in 2004, although it was originally served as a long drink. (A "long" drink is served on ice with the addition of soda water.) The drink was inspired by the newly released Hendrick's gin. The Eastside became more popular after Christy Pope started serving it at Milk & Honey, refining the recipe by serving it "up" (in a stemmed cocktail glass with no ice) and without soda water.

2–3 **cucumber slices**

6–8 **mint leaves**

2 oz (60ml) **gin** (Hendrick's recommended)

1 oz (30ml) freshly squeezed **lime juice**

¾ oz (22.5ml) **simple syrup** (page 28)

1   In a cocktail shaker, gently muddle the cucumber and mint.

2   Add the gin, lime juice, and simple syrup.

3   Add ice and shake for 10 to 12 seconds.

4   Double strain into a chilled coupe glass.

5   Garnish with cucumber and/or mint sprig.

When served on ice, this drink is known as an Old Maid.

*If you like the Eastside, try the **Irish Maid** (page 76), which calls for a combination of whiskey and elderflower liqueur.*

ORIGINATED	TYPE	METHOD	GLASSWARE	GARNISH
2001	Sour	Shaken	Old-fashioned glass	Green grapes

ENZONI

The Enzoni cocktail is a cross between a Negroni and a Gin Sour where the sweet vermouth comes in the form of muddled green grapes. First created by Vincenzo "Enzo" Errico whilst tending bar at Milk & Honey in New York, the Enzoni is an ideal drink to introduce a novice to the world of Campari. Vincenzo was trained by the legendary Dick Bradsell, creator of the **Espresso Martini** (page 284), and he also created a Brooklyn variation called the **Red Hook** (page 96).

5 **green grapes**

1 oz (30ml) **gin**

1 oz (30ml) **Campari**

¾ oz (22.5ml) freshly squeezed **lemon juice**

½ oz (15ml) **simple syrup** (page 28)

1   In a cocktail shaker, muddle the grapes.

2   Add the remaining ingredients.

3   Add ice and shake for 10 to 12 seconds.

4   Strain over fresh ice into an old-fashioned glass.

5   Garnish with 3 skewered grapes.

Don't have grapes? Try your luck with other fruit or berries!

ORIGINATED	TYPE	METHOD	GLASSWARE	GARNISH
1927	Fizz	Shaken	Champagne flute	Lemon twist

FRENCH 75

The French 75 was first seen in print in a 1927 book called *Here's How!* and three years later it was included in *The Savoy Cocktail Book*, which enabled its spread and cemented its popularity. There's mention of the same combination of ingredients being mixed together in Boston as far back as 1867, but it wasn't referred to as a French 75.

The drink is commonly served up in a champagne flute, although I often prefer to serve it in a highball glass over ice. Cognac in place of gin is also a welcome variation, and I highly recommend comparing the two.

1½ oz (45ml) **gin**

¾ oz (22.5ml) freshly squeezed **lemon juice**

¾ oz (22.5ml) **simple syrup** (page 28)

3 oz (90ml) **dry champagne**

1 In a cocktail shaker, combine the gin, lemon juice, and simple syrup.

2 Add ice and shake for 10 to 12 seconds.

3 Gently add the champagne to the cocktail shaker.

4 Double strain into a chilled champagne flute.

Try both the gin and cognac versions side by side to discover your favourite.

ORIGINATED	TYPE	METHOD	GLASSWARE	GARNISH
Circa 1917	Sour	Shaken	Coupe glass	Lime wheel

GIMLET

According to cocktail historian David Wondrich, the Gimlet's history goes back to 1867 when the British government mandated that merchant ships would stock rations of lime juice to prevent scurvy. Rose's Sweetened Lime Juice was patented and released in the same year, but it wasn't until 1917 that the Gimlet was mentioned in print.

Traditionally, the recipe called for equal parts of navy-strength gin (57.15% ABV) and Rose's Sweetened Lime Juice, but it's commonly made in the same manner as a **Daiquiri** (page 200) with fresh ingredients (gin, lime, and simple syrup).

2 oz (60ml) **London dry** or **Plymouth gin**

⅔ oz (20ml) **lime cordial** (page 31)

1   In a cocktail shaker, combine all ingredients.

2   Add ice and shake for 10 to 12 seconds.

3   Double strain into a chilled coupe glass.

4   Garnish with a lime wheel, if desired.

If you don't have time to make a cordial, you can make a fresh version of the Gimlet with 2 ounces (60ml) gin, ⅔ ounce (20ml) freshly squeezed lime juice, and ½ ounce (15ml) simple syrup.

ORIGINATED	TYPE	METHOD	GLASSWARE	GARNISH
Late 1800s	Highball	Built	Highball glass	Citrus wedge

GIN + TONIC

The Gin & Tonic dates back to the late 1800s when British soldiers would mix gin with their quinine water. Quinine water, also known as tonic water, was originally consumed as a medicinal beverage to avoid contracting malaria. The antimalarial ingredient in tonic—quinine—is an extract from the bark of a tree native to South America.

Typically a British highball, it is now immensely popular throughout the world for its simplicity and unique taste. Common ratios range from 2 to 4 parts tonic water to 1 part gin.

Choose your favourite gin and pair it with a high-quality tonic water such as Fever-Tree.

1 oz (30ml) **gin**

4 oz (120ml) **tonic water**

1   Fill a highball (or old-fashioned) glass with ice.

2   Add the gin and top with tonic water.

3   Garnish with a wedge of citrus.

Choose your garnish based on the botanicals featured in your gin. One of my favourite gins, Threefold Aromatic Gin, features grapefruit, rosemary, and lavender as the hero botanicals, so a garnish of ruby red grapefruit and a sprig of rosemary enhances the gin's flavour profile.

ORIGINATED	TYPE	METHOD	GLASSWARE	GARNISH
1870	Daisy	Shaken	Old-fashioned glass	Lemon wheel

GIN DAISY

The original Daisy of the 1870s was a mix of spirit, orange cordial, lemon juice, and soda water. There are a myriad of variations for the Daisy, including alternate base spirits such as gin, brandy, rum, or whiskey. The orange cordial is often replaced with orange curaçao, raspberry syrup, grenadine, maraschino liqueur, orgeat, or even Yellow Chartreuse. However, the classic Gin Daisy has been the most popular choice of Daisy over the last century.

2 oz (60ml) **gin**

¾ oz (22.5ml) **orange liqueur**

¾ oz (22.5ml) freshly squeezed **lemon juice**

1 oz (30ml) **soda water**

1   In a cocktail shaker, combine all ingredients.

2   Add ice and shake for 10 to 12 seconds.

3   Strain over fresh ice into an old-fashioned glass.

4   Add a dash of soda water and garnish with a lemon wheel.

Try using the ingredients mentioned in the description to create your own unique take on a Daisy!

ORIGINATED	TYPE	METHOD	GLASSWARE	GARNISH
Circa 2005	Sour	Shaken	Highball or Collins glass	Mint sprig, lime wheel, candied ginger

GIN GIN MULE

The Gin Gin Mule is an Audrey Saunders creation, developed during her time as owner of the recently closed yet influential Pegu Club in New York City. Both the Pegu Club and Audrey had a huge impact on the modern cocktail renaissance. She is well known amongst her industry peers and has created many modern classics in addition to the Gin Gin Mule, including the **Earl Grey MarTEAni** (page 132) and the Intro to Aperol.

A slightly spicy but refreshing drink, the Gin Gin Mule is a cross between a **Mojito** (page 216) and a **Moscow Mule** (page 288) made with gin. Audrey considers homemade, uncarbonated ginger beer nonnegotiable as it contains less sugar than store-bought varieties. If you utilise a store-bought ginger beer, opt for one that is dry and add it to the finished drink rather than prior to shaking.

1 **mint sprig**

1 oz (30ml) **simple syrup** (page 28)

1¾ oz (52.5ml) **gin**

¾ oz (22.5ml) freshly squeezed **lime juice**

1 oz (30ml) **ginger beer** (page 31)

1   In a cocktail shaker, gently muddle the mint with the simple syrup.

2   Add the gin, lime juice, and uncarbonated ginger beer.

3   Add ice and shake for 10 to 12 seconds.

4   Strain over fresh ice into a Collins glass.

5   Garnish with a mint sprig, a lime wheel, and candied ginger.

You may need to reduce the amount of simple syrup if you choose to use a store-bought ginger beer.

ORIGINATED	TYPE	METHOD	GLASSWARE	GARNISH
Early 1900s	Vermouth cocktail	Stirred	Coupe glass	Orange twist

HANKY PANKY

The Hanky Panky was created by Ada Coleman, one of the female powerhouses of the early cocktail bar scene, during her time at the Savoy Hotel's American Bar in London from 1903 to 1926. She created the drink for one of the many celebrities she regularly served, an English actor who went by the name of Sir Charles Hawtrey. Upon trying the drink for the first time he exclaimed, "By Jove! That is the real hanky-panky!" which is how the drink inevitably got its name.

Coleman was the only female head bartender to lead the team at the American Bar and left a strong legacy on the cocktail world. She also mentored Harry Craddock, author of *The Savoy Cocktail Book*.

2 oz (60ml) **gin**

1½ oz (45ml) **sweet vermouth**

¼ oz (7.5ml) **Fernet Branca**

1 In a mixing glass, combine all the ingredients.

2 Add ice and stir for 15 to 30 seconds.

3 Strain into a chilled coupe glass.

4 Garnish with an orange twist.

*If you enjoy the format of this cocktail but can't embrace the bold flavours of Fernet Branca, then why not try a **Martinez** (page 156)? It's similar in style, but the Fernet is replaced with a maraschino liqueur.*

ORIGINATED	TYPE	METHOD	GLASSWARE	GARNISH
2021	Sour	Shaken	Nick and Nora glass	Strawberry half

KING'S BREAKFAST

I love the classics. They have stood the test of time, which means they are a great place to start when creating your own unique variations. The King's Breakfast is an example of this. It uses the Breakfast Martini as a template, but substitutes strawberry jam in place of marmalade and splits the base between gin and Italicus Rosolio di Bergamotto liqueur. The resulting cocktail is unique, bright, and citrusy, highlighting the citrus notes of Threefold Aromatic Gin and the floral aspect of Italicus.

¾ oz (22.5ml) **Italicus Rosolio di Bergamotto**

¾ oz (22.5ml) **gin** (Threefold Aromatic recommended)

¾ oz (22.5ml) freshly squeezed **lemon juice**

1 tsp **strawberry jam,** heaped

1 In a cocktail shaker, combine all ingredients.

2 Add ice and shake for 10 to 12 seconds.

3 Double strain into a chilled Nick and Nora glass.

4 Garnish with a strawberry half.

The recipe was developed using a two simple techniques for creating a new cocktail: splitting the base ingredient and "Mr. Potato Head." Try creating your own house cocktail using the methods described on pages 42–43.

ORIGINATED	TYPE	METHOD	GLASSWARE	GARNISH
1920s	Sour	Shaken	Coupe glass	Maraschino cherry

LAST WORD

The Last Word was created in the early 1920s at the Detroit Athletic Club. The cocktail was only popular for a few decades and was later published by Ted Saucier in his 1951 book *Bottoms Up*.

A Seattle bartender named Murray Stenson revived the cocktail by placing it on his drinks menu in 2003. Its popularity in Seattle helped the drink find its way onto the menu at the Pegu Club, which cemented its resurgence and became a cult classic.

¾ oz (22.5ml) **gin**

¾ oz (22.5ml) **Green Chartreuse**

¾ oz (22.5ml) **maraschino liqueur** (Luxardo recommended)

¾ oz (22.5ml) freshly squeezed **lime juice**

1 In a cocktail shaker, combine all ingredients.

2 Add ice and shake for 10 to 12 seconds.

3 Double strain into a chilled coupe glass.

4 Garnish with a maraschino cherry.

You can play around with the gin component—substitute an Irish whiskey for a Dublin Minstrel or mezcal for a Last of the Oaxacans. There are an endless number of riffs on the Last Word.

ORIGINATED	TYPE	METHOD	GLASSWARE	GARNISH
2002	Sour	Shaken	Coupe glass	Grapefruit twist

LONDON CALLING

The London Calling was created by Chris Jepson at Milk & Honey, London in 2002. Well, sort of. A cocktail composed of the same ingredients—the Barbara West Cocktail—has existed since the 1930s. Whilst that drink had been around for more than 70 years before Chris' creation, it never gained mainstream popularity. Chris refined the ratios and replaced the Angostura bitters with orange bitters, and his version went on to become a bartender favourite during a sherry resurgence.

1½ oz (45ml) **London dry gin**

½ oz (15ml) **fino sherry**

½ oz (15ml) freshly squeezed **lemon juice**

½ oz (15ml) **simple syrup** (page 28)

2 dashes of **orange bitters**

1 In a cocktail shaker, combine all ingredients.

2 Add ice and shake for 10 to 12 seconds.

3 Double strain into a chilled coupe glass.

4 Garnish with a grapefruit twist.

Other dry sherry options are Manzanilla, Amontillado, or Oloroso Don't have any sherry? Use a dry vermouth in its place.

ORIGINATED	TYPE	METHOD	GLASSWARE	GARNISH
1884	Vermouth cocktails	Stirred	Coupe glass	Lemon twist

MARTINEZ

The Martinez evolved from the Turf Club cocktail, which emerged in the 1870s. The first written reference of the Turf Club was a simple mix of Old Tom gin and sweet vermouth in equal portions with a few dashes of Peruvian bitters. Maraschino liqueur was a common modifier at the time, so it didn't take long to make its way into the Turf Club, resulting in the Martinez.

1½ oz (45ml) **Old Tom gin**

¾ oz (22.5ml) **sweet vermouth**

1 tsp (5ml) **maraschino liqueur** (Luxardo recommended)

1 dash of **Angostura bitters**

1 dash of **orange bitters**

1   In a mixing glass, combine all ingredients.

2   Add ice and stir for 15 to 30 seconds.

3   Strain into a chilled coupe glass.

4   Garnish with a twist of lemon.

Dutch genever can be used in place of the Old Tom gin for a more malty, whiskey-esque version.

ORIGINATED	TYPE	METHOD	GLASSWARE	GARNISH
1904	Vermouth cocktail	Stirred	Stemmed cocktail glass	Olive

MARTINI (DRY)

The first written reference to a Dry Martini was in 1904, although it was listed with a 50/50 split of gin and dry vermouth, which differs from the bone dry versions of today. Some older references to the Martini call for a dash of syrup so the term "dry" historically referred to the omission of the syrup. Many older written recipes also called for sweet vermouth and curaçao which brings it far closer to Martinez territory.

There are a number of alternate styles of martini including the Dirty Martini, with olive brine; the Perfect Martini, with both sweet and dry vermouth; and the Fitty-Fitty, with an equal split of gin and dry vermouth.

2½ oz (75ml) **dry gin**
½ oz (15ml) **dry vermouth**
1 dash of **orange bitters**

1   In a mixing glass, combine all ingredients.

2   Add ice and stir for 20 to 40 seconds.

3   Strain into a chilled stemmed cocktail glass.

4   Express a lemon peel over the top and discard.

5   Garnish with an olive (or lemon twist).

Savoury gins are an excellent choice in a Martini. (Threefold Mediterranean Gin, perhaps?)

Try playing with different martini ratios. Using less vermouth results in a drier drink.

ORIGINATED	TYPE	METHOD	GLASSWARE	GARNISH
Circa 1920	Vermouth cocktail	Built	Old-fashioned glass	Orange wedge

NEGRONI

Legend has it that an Italian count named Camillo Negroni ordered a gin-fortified Americano at Café Casoni in Florence in 1920. It went on to become his "usual" drink.

Things went quiet for the Negroni during Mussolini's reign from 1922 to 1943, as foreign practices such as drinking cocktails were strongly frowned upon and even the word "cocktail" was banned. The Negroni wasn't seen in print until 1947, when it appeared in Amedeo Gandiglio's *Cocktails Portfolio*. His written version closely resembles how it is served today—equal parts gin, sweet vermouth, and Campari, served on the rocks with a twist of orange (albeit with a dash of seltzer).

The equal part recipe is the "classic" Negroni recipe, although an altered ratio in favour of the gin– or a higher-proof gin–works exceptionally well.

1¼ oz (37.5ml) **gin**

1 oz (30ml) **Campari**

1 oz (30ml) **sweet vermouth**

1   In an old-fashioned glass, combine all ingredients.

2   Fill the glass with ice and stir briefly.

3   Express an orange peel over the top and discard.

4   Garnish with an orange wedge.

Try experimenting with accents such as a few dashes of chocolate bitters.

Replacing the gin with Smith & Cross Jamaican overproof rum turns the drink into a Kingston Negroni (and preferably use Carpano Antica Formula for the sweet vermouth).

ORIGINATED	TYPE	METHOD	GLASSWARE	GARNISH
1920s	Daisy	Shaken	Stemmed cocktail glass	Lime twist

PEGU CLUB

The Pegu Club was created in Yangon, Myanmar (formerly Burma) at none other than the Pegu Club, a gentlemen's club for British officers formed in the 1880s. The drink was later featured in Harry McElhone's *Barflies and Cocktails* in 1927 before being resurrected by Audrey Saunders in the mid-2000s when she placed it on her menu at the Pegu Club in New York City.

2 oz (60ml) **gin**

¾ oz (22.5ml) **dry curaçao**

¾ oz (22.5ml) freshly squeezed **lime juice**

1 dash of **Angostura bitters**

1 dash of **orange bitters**

1 In a cocktail shaker, combine all ingredients.

2 Add ice and shake for 10 to 12 seconds.

3 Double strain into a chilled stemmed cocktail glass.

4 Garnish with a lime twist.

This is a dry cocktail. Experiment with orange liqueurs if you prefer something sweeter.

ORIGINATED	TYPE	METHOD	GLASSWARE	GARNISH
1888	Fizz	Shaken	Highball glass	None

RAMOS GIN FIZZ

The Ramos Gin Fizz was first mixed by Henry Charles Ramos in 1888 at the Imperial Cabinet Saloon in New Orleans. The light, fresh, and floral drink is one of the city's most well-known cocktails.

Originally, it took over 12 minutes of shaking to achieve the drink's signature foamy consistency, which led Henry to hire a team of bartenders to shake the cocktail one by one. The meringue-like foam can be easily replicated in a few minutes by following these tips: 1) ensure you dry shake to emulsify the egg white; 2) shake vigorously; 3) chill your glass, preferably in the freezer; and 4) let the drink settle before topping with soda.

Follow these tips, and the thick foam will elevate above the rim of the glass and be sturdy enough to hold a stainless steel straw in an upright position.

2 oz (60ml) **Old Tom gin**

1 oz (30ml) **heavy cream**

½ oz (15ml) freshly squeezed **lime juice**

½ oz (15ml) freshly squeezed **lemon juice**

½ oz (15ml) **simple syrup** (page 28)

½ oz (15ml) **egg white**

1 dash of **orange blossom water**

1 oz (30ml) **soda water,** plus more to top

1 In a cocktail shaker, combine all ingredients except the soda water.

2 Dry shake (without ice) for 5 to 10 seconds.

3 Add ice and shake vigorously for 10 to 12 seconds.

4 To a chilled highball glass, add 1 oz (30ml) soda water.

5 Slowly strain the drink into the highball glass.

6 Place the drink in the refrigerator or freezer to settle for up to 2 minutes.

7 Top with more soda water and finish with a stainless steel straw in the middle.

For an even fluffier Ramos Gin Fizz, use a milkshake maker instead of shaking.

ORIGINATED	TYPE	METHOD	GLASSWARE	GARNISH
1967	Tropical	Flash blended	Old-fashioned glass	Cherry, lime twist

SATURN

The Saturn is one of the few tropical cocktails that features gin as the base spirit. The original recipe is served as a frozen cocktail (blended with ice) but I much prefer a flash-blended version with crushed or pebble ice for a more intense passionfruit and citrus flavour.

The drink is credited to Californian bartender J. "Popo" Galsini, who won the 1967 International Bartender's Association World Championship with his recipe.

1½ oz (45ml) **gin**

½ oz (15ml) freshly squeezed **lemon juice**

½ oz (15ml) **passion fruit syrup**

¼ oz (7.5ml) **falernum**

¼ oz (7.5ml) **orgeat** (page 30)

1 To a milkshake maker tin, add all ingredients.

2 Add pebble ice and flash blend.

3 Transfer to an old-fashioned glass and top with more pebble ice, if needed.

4 Garnish with a skewered maraschino cherry and lime peel.

Craft your garnish to look like Saturn, with the cherry as the planet and the lime peel representing the rings.

If you don't have a milkshake maker, you can whip shake this drink (see page 38).

ORIGINATED	TYPE	METHOD	GLASSWARE	GARNISH
1876	Fizz	Shaken	Fizz glass	None

SILVER FIZZ

Jerry Thomas first wrote about the Fizz in 1876, and much like the Daisy, gin was a popular spirit choice. The Silver Fizz is akin to the **Tom Collins** (page 175), with the key differences being that it includes an egg white, is served in a fizz glass (6–8 oz) with no ice, and is designed to be consumed promptly.

As with many classic cocktails, there are a number of different ways you may choose to go with a Fizz. Adding an egg yolk will make a Golden Fizz, and a whole egg will make a Royal Fizz, but perhaps one of the most famous of Fizzes would be the **Ramos Gin Fizz** (page 164) which contains egg white, cream, and orange blossom water.

2 oz (60ml) **gin**

¾ oz (22.5ml) freshly squeezed **lemon juice**

¾ oz (22.5ml) **simple syrup** (page 28)

½ oz (15ml) **egg white**

1–2 oz (30–60ml) **soda water**

1   In a cocktail shaker, combine the gin, lemon juice, simple syrup, and egg white.

2   Dry shake (without ice) for 5 to 10 seconds.

3   Add ice and shake for 10 to 12 seconds.

4   Double strain into a chilled fizz or highball glass.

5   Slowly add soda water to carbonate.

Why not add your own flavour to your Fizz? Muddle some fresh fruit in the cocktail shaker before measuring in the other ingredients. Strawberries, raspberries, or other seasonal fruit can be used.

ORIGINATED	TYPE	METHOD	GLASSWARE	GARNISH
Circa 1915	Tropical	Shaken	Highball glass	Cherry, orange slice

SINGAPORE SLING

The Singapore Sling is said to have originated at the Long Bar of the iconic Raffles Hotel in Singapore. The drink was popular for the years that followed, but it went out of fashion in the 1930s. Ngiam Tong Boon's original recipe was lost for decades, and it wasn't until the 1970s that a copy of the recipe was resurrected by his nephew and supplied to the hotel.

The hotel's Singapore Sling recipe calls for a whopping four ounces of pineapple juice, but I recommend an adapted version in which the pineapple juice is replaced with soda water. (Some would argue soda water is included in the true original recipe.) As with countless cocktails, the original recipe is often debated.

1½ oz (45ml) **London Dry gin**

½ oz (15ml) **Heering cherry liqueur**

¼ oz (7.5ml) **Benedictine**

¾ oz (22.5ml) freshly squeezed **lemon juice**

¼ oz (7.5ml) **grenadine** (page 30)

1 dash of **Angostura bitters**

1 dash of **orange bitters**

2 oz (60ml) **soda water**

1   In a cocktail shaker, combine all ingredients except the soda water.

2   Add ice and shake for 10 to 12 seconds.

3   Add the soda water to the shaker and strain over fresh ice into a highball glass.

4   Garnish with a skewered maraschino cherry and an orange slice.

Try the recipe with pineapple juice and omit the soda water for a sweet and fluffy Singapore Sling.

ORIGINATED	TYPE	METHOD	GLASSWARE	GARNISH
1916	Sour	Shaken	Coupe glass	Mint sprig

SOUTHSIDE

The Southside was first referenced as a "South Side Fizz" in Hugo Ensslin's *Recipes for Mixed Drinks*. The recipe was listed simply as "Made same as Gin Fizz, adding fresh mint leaves" but over time the fizz aspect has fallen out of favour and it's the Southside served up (without soda water) that is the most popular version today.

Many bartenders skew toward either lemon or lime juice for their Southside, but I've split the difference and called for a half measure of each, which is also more true to Hugo's written recipe.

4–6 **mint leaves**

¾ oz (22.5 ml) **simple syrup** (page 28)

2 oz (60 ml) **gin**

½ oz (15 ml) freshly squeezed **lemon juice**

½ oz (15 ml) freshly squeezed **lime juice**

1   In a cocktail shaker, gently muddle the mint and simple syrup.

2   Add the remaining ingredients.

3   Add ice and shake for 10 to 12 seconds.

4   Double strain into a chilled coupe glass.

5   Garnish with a mint sprig.

Serve in a tall glass with a spritz of soda water for a Southside Fizz.

ORIGINATED	TYPE	METHOD	GLASSWARE	GARNISH
1870s	Collins	Shaken	Collins glass	Lemon wedge

TOM COLLINS

The Tom Collins was first seen in Jerry Thomas' *The Bartender's Guide* in 1876. Other versions of the Collins date back further, but these were most likely made using Dutch genever rather than gin. The drink is named after John Collins, a waiter in London who was famous for his gin punch.

2 oz (60ml) **Old Tom gin**

¾ oz (22.5ml) freshly squeezed **lemon juice**

½ oz (15ml) **simple syrup** (page 28)

2 oz (60ml) **soda water**

1 In a cocktail shaker, combine the gin, lemon juice, and simple syrup.

2 Add ice and shake for 10 to 12 seconds.

3 Add the soda water to the shaker and strain over fresh ice into a Collins glass.

4 Garnish with a lemon wedge.

Don't have any Old Tom gin? Try an alternate gin or spirit, such as whiskey.

ORIGINATED	TYPE	METHOD	GLASSWARE	GARNISH
2011	Sour	Shaken	Coupe glass	None

TOO SOON?

This contemporary cocktail was created by Sam Ross of Attaboy, New York. It features bright, fresh, citrusy top notes that evolve into bitter citrus and subtle vegetal flavours courtesy of the Cynar. Sam is also the creator of modern classic cocktails such as the **Penicillin** (page 95), the **Paper Plane** (page 92), and the **Conquistador** (page 244).

1 oz (30ml) **gin**

1 oz (30ml) **Cynar**

¾ oz (22.5ml) freshly squeezed **lemon juice**

½ oz (15ml) **simple syrup** (page 28)

2 **orange slices**

1   In a cocktail shaker, combine all ingredients.

2   Add ice and shake for 10 to 12 seconds.

3   Double strain into a chilled coupe glass.

If you enjoy the bitter and citrusy combo of the Too Soon?, check out the **Enzoni** *(page 136)*

ORIGINATED	TYPE	METHOD	GLASSWARE	GARNISH
2007	Sour	Shaken	Coupe glass	Lemon twist

WATER LILY

The Water Lily was created by Richard Boccaro in 2007 during his time at Little Branch in New York City. Richard was Sasha Petraske's business partner in the pioneering Queens bar Dutch Kills. He created the drink for Sasha's wife, Georgette Moger-Petraske, who asked for something containing violet syrup and gin.

The violette syrup featured in Sasha Petraske's *Regarding Cocktails* is made of gin, violet syrup (such as Monin), and simple syrup in a 2:1:1 ratio. Alternatively, you could very easily substitute for a créme de violette but the ratios may need to be adjusted.

¾ oz (22.5ml) **gin**

¾ oz (22.5ml) **Cointreau**

¾ oz (22.5ml) **violet syrup**

¾ oz (22.5ml) freshly squeezed **lemon juice**

1 In a cocktail shaker, combine all ingredients.

2 Add ice and shake for 10 to 12 seconds.

3 Double strain into a chilled coupe glass.

4 Garnish with a lemon twist.

If you enjoyed this but prefer citrus over floral notes, the **Corpse Reviver No. 2** *(page 128) is for you!*

ORIGINATED	TYPE	METHOD	GLASSWARE	GARNISH
1929	Sour	Shaken	Coupe glass	Lemon twist

WHITE LADY

The first White Lady was created by Harry MacElhone in 1919. It was a mix of Cointreau, créme de menthe, and brandy—far different from the recipe we know today.

There are three potential creators of the more familiar version, but it was most closely associated with the bar at London's Savoy Hotel and Harry Craddock, who later published it in *The Savoy Cocktail Book* in 1930.

2 oz (60ml) **gin**

¾ oz (22.5ml) **Cointreau**

¾ oz (22.5ml) freshly squeezed **lemon juice**

¼ oz (7.5ml) **simple syrup** (page 26)

½ oz (15ml) **egg white**

1   In a cocktail shaker, combine all ingredients.

2   Dry shake (without ice) for 5 to 10 seconds.

3   Add ice and shake for 10 to 12 seconds.

4   Double strain into a chilled coupe glass.

5   Garnish with a lemon twist.

To make Harry MacElhone's original version, shake 1 ounce (30ml) Cointreau, ½ ounce (15ml) créme de menthe, and ½ ounce (15ml) brandy before straining into a chilled cocktail glass.

ORIGINATED	TYPE	METHOD	GLASSWARE	GARNISH
2002	Vermouth cocktail	Stirred	Old-fashioned	Lemon twist

WHITE NEGRONI

The White Negroni is a cocktail created out of necessity. A British bartender, Wayne Collins, was in Bordeaux, France and didn't have access to the Campari and sweet vermouth needed to make a classic Negroni. In their place, he substituted French aperitifs—Suze gentian liqueur and Lillet Blanc— for a more woody, earthy drink that is less bitter than a traditional Negroni.

2 oz (60ml) **gin**

1 oz (30m) **Lillet Blanc**

¾ oz (22.5ml) **Suze**

1   In an old-fashioned glass, combine all ingredients.

2   Fill the glass with ice and stir for 15 to 30 seconds.

3   Express an orange peel over the top and discard.

4   Garnish with a twist of lemon.

If the woody and earthy characteristics of the gentian seem overpowering, you can reduce the Suze to ½ ounce (15ml) for a brighter drink.

ORIGINATED	TYPE	METHOD	GLASSWARE	GARNISH
1937	Tropical	Flash blended	Coupe glass	Mint sprig

AKU AKU

The Aku Aku was created by Trader Vic and is only a subtle tweak on the Missionary's Downfall, which was created by Donn Beach (a.k.a. Don the Beachcomber). Donn spent some of his formative years in the Caribbean and learned from the region's bartenders. It's believed that he drew inspiration for the Missionary's Downfall from Cuban bartenders who were creating elaborate variations on the **Daiquiri** (page 200).

The Aku Aku replaces the honey syrup used in the Missionary's Downfall with demerara syrup (or simple syrup). Many people prefer to serve it as a blended frozen drink, but I prefer it strained and served up.

5 fresh **pineapple chunks,** about 1-in (2.5cm) cubes

1½ oz (45ml) **lightly aged rum**

½ oz (15ml) **peach liqueur**

1 oz (30ml) freshly squeezed **lime juice**

¾ oz (22.5ml) **demerara syrup** (page 28)

8 **mint leaves**

1   In a milkshake maker tin, muddle the pineapple.

2   Add the remaining ingredients.

3   Add pebble ice and flash blend.

4   Double strain into a chilled coupe glass.

5   Garnish with a mint sprig.

If you don't have peach liqueur on hand, apricot brandy can be a good substitute.

If you don't have a milkshake maker, you can whip shake this drink (see page 38).

ORIGINATED	TYPE	METHOD	GLASSWARE	GARNISH
1920s	Tropical	Shaken	Balloon or hurricane glass	Orange slice, pineapple spear, grated nutmeg

ANGOSTURA COLADA

The Angostura Colada follows the format of a **Piña Colada** (page 224) with rum, pineapple, and coconut, but there are a few key differences. Zac Overman's creation employs heavy use of Angostura bitters, resulting in a unique colada. He prefers Smith & Cross overproof Jamaican rum, which creates a foundation of exotic fruit and spice, whilst the large measure of bitters adds a complex array of spices such as cinnamon and clove.

The drink is still a tropical colada at heart but with more intricate flavours of fruit and spice.

1½ oz (45ml) **Angostura bitters**

½ oz (15ml) aged **Jamaican rum** (Smith & Cross recommended)

2 oz (60ml) **pineapple juice**

1½ oz (45ml) **cream of coconut** (page 30)

1 oz (30ml) freshly squeezed **lime juice**

1   In a cocktail shaker, combine all ingredients.

2   Add ice and shake for 10 to 12 seconds.

3   Strain over pebble ice into a balloon glass.

4   Garnish with a slice of orange, a pineapple spear, and freshly grated nutmeg.

Store your pineapple spears in the freezer for an easy go-to garnish.

ORIGINATED	TYPE	METHOD	GLASSWARE	GARNISH
2015	Tropical	Shaken	Old-fashioned glass	Mint Sprig

ARTICHOKE HOLD

The Artichoke Hold was created by Jeremy Oertel from the Brooklyn cocktail bar Donna. It's a riff on one of his other creations, the **Bitter Mai Tai** (page 191), which in turn is a riff on a classic **Mai Tai** (page 215). The funkiness of the Smith & Cross rum creates the base whilst the Cynar and elderflower liqueur add an interesting bittersweet combination of flavours.

¾ oz (22.5ml) aged **Jamaican rum** (Smith & Cross recommended)

¾ oz (22.5ml) **Cynar**

½ oz (15ml) **St-Germain elderflower liqueur**

¾ oz (22.5ml) freshly squeezed **lime juice**

½ oz (15ml) **orgeat** (page 30)

1   In a cocktail shaker, combine all ingredients.

2   Add ice and shake for 10 to 12 seconds.

3   Strain over pebble ice into an old-fashioned glass.

4   Garnish with a mint sprig.

You can opt to substitute an alternate Jamaican pot still rum, although Smith & Cross does bring a unique flavour profile.

ORIGINATED	TYPE	METHOD	GLASSWARE	GARNISH
2011	Tropical	Shaken	Old-fashioned glass	Mint sprig

BITTER MAI TAI

The Bitter Mai Tai is a creation of Jeremy Oertel, creator of several modern classics including the **Artichoke Hold** (page 188) and **Brancolada** (page 192).

Jeremy threw a party alongside notable tiki bartender Brian Miller whilst in Williamsburg and wanted to replicate a Mai Tai variation he'd come across that used Angostura bitters in place of rum. Angostura can be expensive in large quantities, so he used a combination of Campari and Smith & Cross Jamaican rum for a funky, spicy, and bitter combination.

1½ oz (45ml) **Campari**

¾ oz (22.5ml) aged **Jamaican rum** (Smith & Cross recommended)

½ oz (15ml) **dry curaçao**

1 oz (30ml) freshly squeezed **lime juice**

¾ oz (22.5ml) **orgeat** (page 30)

1 In a cocktail shaker, combine all ingredients.

2 Add ice and shake for 10 to 12 seconds.

3 Strain over pebble ice into an old-fashioned glass.

4 Garnish with a mint sprig.

*Make sure you try the classic **Mai Tai** (page 215)!*

ORIGINATED	TYPE	METHOD	GLASSWARE	GARNISH
2012	Tropical	Flash blended	Hurricane or balloon glass	Orange slice, mint sprig

BRANCOLADA

The Brancolada was created by Jeremy Oertel, who worked at several notable New York bars including Death & Co., Dram, and Donna. The drink is a delicious variation on the classic Piña Colada. It calls for the addition of Branca Menta, an intensely minty liqueur, which adds intricate yet subtle bitterness and herbal characteristics.

The bar team at Dram would drizzle chilled Branca Menta over ice cream sandwiches, which inspired Jeremy's summery dessert drink. The drink was served frozen from a slushie machine at Donna bar in Brooklyn, where it gained a cult following.

1 oz (30ml) **Branca Menta**

1 oz (30ml) aged **Jamaican rum**

1½ oz (45ml) **pineapple juice**

¾ oz (22.5ml) **cream of coconut** (page 30)

¼ oz (7.5ml) freshly squeezed **orange juice**

1   In a milkshake maker tin, combine all ingredients.

2   Add pebble ice and flash blend.

3   Pour into a hurricane or balloon glass and top with more pebble ice.

4   Garnish with a mint sprig and slice of orange.

Enjoy frozen drinks? Serve it like Donna and blend it with ice.

If you don't have a milkshake maker, you can whip shake this drink (see page 38).

ORIGINATED	TYPE	METHOD	GLASSWARE	GARNISH
1996	Daisy	Shaken	Coupe glass	Cinnamon sugar rim

CABLE CAR

The Cable Car was created by Tony Abou-Ganim in 1996 as the signature cocktail of the Starlight Room at the Drake Hotel in San Francisco. At its core, it is a simple variation on the classic **Sidecar** (page 275), calling for spiced rum in place of cognac.

Cinnamon sugar, to rim the glass

1½ oz (45ml) **spiced rum**

¾ oz (22.5ml) **orange curaçao**

1 oz (30ml) freshly squeezed **lemon juice**

½ oz (15ml) **simple syrup** (page 28)

1 Rim a chilled coupe glass with cinnamon sugar.

2 In a cocktail shaker, combine all ingredients.

3 Add ice and shake for 10 to 12 seconds.

4 Double strain into the prepared glass.

Experiment with making your own spiced rum by infusing a bottle of rum with whole spices and aromatics such as cinnamon, allspice, clove, nutmeg, ginger, orange peel, and vanilla.

ORIGINATED	TYPE	METHOD	GLASSWARE	GARNISH
1856	Smash	Built	Old-fashioned glass	None

CAIPIRINHA

The Caipirinha hails from Brazil and is the most famous from a category of Brazilian drinks known as Batidas. A traditional Batida consists of cachaça, sugar, fruits, juices, and ice, and is usually shaken in a cocktail shaker or mixed in a blender. Both the Coconut Batida and Passionfruit Batida are also popular in Brazil.

Whilst the three-ingredient drink may appear simple, the preparation is important if you want to keep it authentic. In Brazil, the drink is usually prepared in the glass in which it is served, but it is also common to prepare it in a shaker, giving the drink a short shake prior to transferring to a glass. The former method will result in a stronger drink, whilst the latter will chill, dilute, and soften the spirit.

Many people choose to include simple syrup as the sweetener, but using sugar helps to extract the oils from the skin of the lime and keeps it traditional.

1 whole **lime**

2 tsp superfine **sugar**

2 oz (60ml) **cachaça**

1   Trim the ends off the lime and cut it into quarters from end to end. Remove the white edge from each lime wedge and then cut each wedge in half.

2   In an old-fashioned glass, muddle the lime with the sugar.

3   Add the cachaça and fill the glass with ice. Stir briefly.

Scan the QR code to watch a step-by-step guide to perfect your lime preparation.

Don't have cachaça on hand? Try it with a lightly aged rum (for a Caipirissima) or vodka (for a Caipiroska).

ORIGINATED	TYPE	METHOD	GLASSWARE	GARNISH
1900s	Highball	Built	Highball glass	Lime wedge

CUBA LIBRE

The legend of the Cuba Libre goes back to 1900, when an American captain stationed in Havana during the Spanish-American War poured a drink combining Bacardi, Coca-Cola, and a squeeze of fresh lime before crying out, *"Por Cuba libre!"* ("To a free Cuba!")

Although Bacardi has claimed the Cuba Libre as its own, the drink can be enjoyed with any light Spanish-style rum.

2 oz (60ml) **lightly aged rum**

1 oz (30ml) freshly squeezed **lime juice**

3 oz (90ml) **cola**

1   Fill a highball glass with ice and add all ingredients.

2   Stir gently to combine and garnish with a lime wedge.

For a more intense lime flavour, muddle a few slices of lime in the glass before adding the ice and building the drink. This will extract some of the oils from the skin of the lime.

ORIGINATED	TYPE	METHOD	GLASSWARE	GARNISH
1898	Sour	Shaken	Coupe glass	None

DAIQUIRI

The Daiquiri is a simple three-ingredient cocktail consisting of rum, lime, and sugar. It was created by Jennings Cox, an American mining engineer, in 1898. Cox named the drink "Daiquiri" after a town in Cuba near the Caribbean Sea. In his diary, Cox wrote, "Put all ingredients in a cocktail shaker and shake well. Do not strain as the glass may be served with some ice," implying that the original was intended to be served over ice, which may have inspired the frozen daiquiri that is familiar to most people today.

The Daiquiri is an excellent drink to experiment with varying ratios and learn about the balance of sweet and sour in mixed drinks. (Refer to page 41 for more information about balancing cocktails.)

2 oz (60ml) **lightly aged rum**

⅔ oz (20ml) freshly squeezed **lime juice**

⅓ oz (10ml) **rich syrup** (page 28)

1   In a cocktail shaker, combine all ingredients.

2   Add ice and shake for 10 to 12 seconds.

3   Double strain into a chilled coupe glass.

The Daiquiri is the perfect vehicle to experiment with different types of rum.

ORIGINATED	TYPE	METHOD	GLASSWARE	GARNISH
2011	Miscellaneous	Stirred	Nick and Nora glass	None

DOMINICANA

Sasha Petraske, the late founder of the famous New York bar Milk & Honey, created the Dominicana around 2011. It is now a staple at The Everleigh in Melbourne, a highly awarded, classic cocktail bar with a purist approach to cocktails and high attention to detail. It's a rich, creamy, and decadent drink—all with just three ingredients.

1½ oz (45ml) aged **Dominican rum**

1½ oz (45ml) **coffee liqueur**

1½ oz (45ml) **heavy cream**

1 In a mixing glass, combine the rum and coffee liqueur.

2 Add ice and stir for 15 to 30 seconds.

3 Strain into a chilled Nick and Nora glass.

4 Gently float the heavy cream on top.

If using a coffee liqueur with a lower sugar content (such as Mr Black), consider adding a dash of simple syrup.

ORIGINATED	TYPE	METHOD	GLASSWARE	GARNISH
Circa 1937	Tropical	Flash blended	Old-fashioned glass	Grated nutmeg

DON'S OWN GROG

Don's Own Grog was created by Donn Beach (a.k.a. Don the Beachcomber) around 1937 and was first featured in *Beachbum Berry's Sippin' Safari* in 2007. It was also adapted and featured in Martin Cate's *Smuggler's Cove*.

Like many tropical drinks, it calls for a combination of several rums to bring complexity, but it is the use of blackberry liqueur (crème de mûre) that sets it apart.

1 oz (30ml) **aged rum**

½ oz (15ml) **lightly aged rum**

½ oz (15ml) **black rum**

½ oz (15ml) **crème de mûre**

¾ oz (22.5ml) freshly squeezed **lime juice**

¼ oz (7.5ml) **demerara syrup** (page 28)

1 dash of **grenadine** (page 30)

1 dash of **Angostura bitters**

1 In a milkshake maker tin, combine all ingredients.

2 Add pebble ice and flash blend.

3 Transfer the contents of the tin to a hurricane or highball glass.

4 Top with more pebble ice and garnish with freshly grated nutmeg.

Don't have all three rums on hand? Try your own blend of rums.

If you don't have a milkshake maker, you can whip shake this drink (see page 38).

ORIGINATED	TYPE	METHOD	GLASSWARE	GARNISH
Circa 1937	Sour	Shaken	Coupe glass	Lime wheel

HEMINGWAY DAIQUIRI

The Hemingway Daiquiri is named for Ernest Hemingway, who enjoyed the drink at El Floridita in Havana, Cuba. As a diabetic, Hemingway preferred to avoid added sugar, which made the original recipe unbalanced. This adapted version is well balanced and highlights the maraschino liqueur.

The Hemingway Daiquiri was typically served over crushed or shaved ice, but it is now commonly served as a blended frozen drink or served up, as is this version.

2 oz (60ml) **lightly aged rum**

¼ oz (7.5ml) **maraschino liqueur**

¾ oz (22.5ml) freshly squeezed **lime juice**

½ oz (15ml) freshly squeezed **grapefruit juice**

¼ oz (7.5ml) **simple syrup** (page 28)

1   In a cocktail shaker, combine all ingredients.

2   Add ice and shake for 10 to 12 seconds.

3   Double strain into a chilled coupe glass.

4   Garnish with a lime wheel.

Try adding a small peel of grapefruit into your drink when shaking. This technique is referred to as the "regal shake."

ORIGINATED	TYPE	METHOD	GLASSWARE	GARNISH
1940s	Tropical	Flash blended	Hurricane glass	Lemon wheel

HURRICANE

The Hurricane originated, surprisingly, at an Irish-themed bar named Pat O'Brien's in New Orleans—not at a renowned tiki bar. It was created out of necessity during the 1940s, when whiskey was in short supply due to the war. Rum was in abundance, and some suppliers would only sell a case of whiskey if it was accompanied by two cases of rum. This meant bars had plenty of rum on hand, which forced them to get creative to move the stock—the Hurricane is a result of this.

The drink is a large, boozy, three-ingredient cocktail consisting of dark Jamaican rum, fresh lemon juice, and passion fruit syrup (or fassionola syrup—a red tropical fruit syrup with prominent notes of passion fruit). Over the decades the drink has changed, and it is often served with orange juice, grenadine, lime juice, and/or simple syrup. Even the Hurricanes served at Pat O'Brien's today are a far cry from the original.

4 oz (120ml) dark **Jamaican rum**

2 oz (60ml) freshly squeezed **lemon juice**

2 oz (60ml) **passion fruit syrup** or fassionola syrup

1 In a milkshake maker tin, combine all ingredients.

2 Add pebble ice and flash blend.

3 Pour into a hurricane glass and top with more pebble ice, if needed.

4 Garnish with a lemon wheel.

Does four ounces of alcohol in one drink seem a bit boozy? Halve the recipe!

If you don't have a milkshake maker, you can whip shake this drink (see page 38).

ORIGINATED	TYPE	METHOD	GLASSWARE	GARNISH
1950s	Tropical	Flash blended	Old-fashioned glass	Lime wheel, maraschino cherry

JET PILOT

The Jet Pilot is even more popular than its predecessor, the Test Pilot (a Don the Beachcomber original). It was created at Stephen Crane's Luau restaurant in Beverly Hills. The restaurant poached some of Don the Beachcomber's bartenders, and as a result, some of their menu items bore a close resemblance to Don's drinks. If you don't have a large selection of rums, you can try replicating with just two varieties such as a light rum and an aged rum.

1 oz (30ml) dark **Jamaican rum**

¾ oz (22.5ml) lightly aged **Puerto Rican rum**

¾ oz (22.5ml) overproof **demerara rum**

½ oz (15ml) **falernum**

½ oz (15ml) **white grapefruit juice**

½ oz (15ml) freshly squeezed **lime juice**

½ oz (15ml) **cinnamon syrup** (see note)

Dash of **Angostura bitters**

Dash of **Herbsaint** or **Pernod**

1   In a milkshake maker tin, combine all ingredients.

2   Add pebble ice and flash blend.

3   Pour into a double old-fashioned glass and top with more pebble ice, if needed.

4   Garnish with a lime wheel and a maraschino cherry.

To make cinnamon syrup, prepare simple syrup as directed on page 28. In a saucepan, heat the syrup over medium-high heat and add 3 cinnamon sticks. When boiling, remove from heat and let steep for 3 to 4 hours before bottling.

ORIGINATED	TYPE	METHOD	GLASSWARE	GARNISH
1973	Tropical	Shaken	Old-fashioned glass	Maraschino cherry, orange, pineapple leaves

JUNGLE BIRD

The Jungle Bird was served as a welcome drink inside the Kuala Lumpur Hilton Hotel's Aviary Bar. Jeffrey Ong created the cocktail, and it was served to guests upon their arrival at the hotel from the time of its opening in 1973. It was first seen in print in *The New American Bartender's Guide* in 1989. The author incorrectly listed the year and creator of the cocktail, which resulted in countless books, blogs, and articles featuring the wrong information, and it wasn't until decades later that the true creator was recognised.

The Jungle Bird saw a resurgence in popularity when Giuseppe González adapted and revived the drink whilst working at Painkiller in New York in the mid-2000s. His recipe reduced the amount of pineapple juice and specified blackstrap rum as the rum of choice. The drink was originally served in a porcelain bird-shaped vessel but is now commonly served in an old-fashioned glass.

1½ oz (45ml) dark **Jamaican rum** or **blackstrap rum**

¾ oz (22.5ml) **Campari**

1½ oz (45ml) **pineapple juice**

½ oz (15ml) freshly squeezed **lime juice**

½ oz (15ml) **simple syrup** (page 28)

1 In a cocktail shaker, combine all ingredients.

2 Add ice and shake for 10 to 12 seconds.

3 Strain over fresh ice into an old-fashioned glass.

4 Garnish with a skewered maraschino, a slice of orange, and 3 pineapple leaves.

If you enjoy bitter tropical drinks, I recommend trying the **Bitter Mai Tai** *(page 191) and the* **Artichoke Hold** *(page 188).*

RUM

ORIGINATED	TYPE	METHOD	GLASSWARE	GARNISH
1944	Tropical	Shaken	Old-fashioned glass	Spent lime, mint sprig

MAI TAI

Trader Vic created the Mai Tai in 1944. Within only a few short years, the popularity of the Mai Tai resulted in limited availability of its key ingredient, Wray & Nephew 17-year Jamaican rum. He chose to substitute the 15-year rum in its place but each time he altered his chosen rum(s), supplies dwindled and he had to adapt his recipe.

First Adjusted Formula: Vic tried stretching his supplies by using only one ounce of the Wray & Nephew 15-year, and the remaining ounce of rum consisted of a blend of two black Jamaican rums (Red Heart and Coruba).

Second Adjusted Formula: Vic later started bottling a Jamaican rum to recreate the original flavour profile, but it was the addition of a Martinique rum (made from molasses, not fresh-pressed cane juice) that made it reminiscent of the original recipe.

The Mai Tai is a favourite amongst rum lovers as it gives the opportunity to experiment with rum blends to make your own perfect Mai Tai.

2 oz (60ml) aged **rum**

½ oz (15ml) **orange curaçao** (Pierre Ferrand Dry Curaçao recommended)

¾ oz (22.5ml) freshly squeezed **lime juice**

½ oz (15ml) **simple syrup** (page 28)

½ oz (15ml) **orgeat** (page 30)

1   In a cocktail shaker, combine all ingredients.

2   Add pebble ice and shake for 10 to 12 seconds.

3   Transfer the contents of the shaker into an old-fashioned glass and top with more ice, if needed.

4   Garnish with the spent lime and a sprig of mint.

Denizen Merchant's Reserve is a blend of rums designed to recreate the flavour profile of Vic's Second Adjusted Formula.

ORIGINATED	TYPE	METHOD	GLASSWARE	GARNISH
Mid-1800s	Collins	Built	Highball glass	Mint sprig

MOJITO

The Mojito is one of Cuba's oldest and most well-known cocktails. The modern version of the drink evolved from the "El Draque," which consisted of aguardiente, mint, and fresh lime. The El Draque was named after the English explorer who visited Havana in 1586, Sir Francis Drake.

When the Original Bacardi company was formed in the mid-1800s, the aguardiente was replaced with rum and the drink was subsequently named the Mojito.

For consistency, I prefer to measure the lime juice rather than muddling the lime, as the size of limes and the amount of juice they produce can vary greatly. If you prefer to muddle lime wedges, add them after the mint so that the lime gets most of the force from muddling. This will extract the oils from the lime skin whilst ensuring the mint doesn't become overly vegetal from heavy muddling.

2 oz (60ml) lightly aged **rum**

1 oz (30ml) freshly squeezed **lime juice**

10–12 **mint leaves**

2 tsp **sugar**

1½ oz (45ml) **soda water**

1 To a highball glass, add the rum, lime juice, mint leaves, and sugar.

2 Gently muddle the mint (bruise the mint but don't over muddle).

3 Add the soda water and top with pebble ice.

4 Garnish with a mint sprig.

Feeling bold? Swap the rum for a smaller measure of Green Chartreuse!

ORIGINATED	TYPE	METHOD	GLASSWARE	GARNISH
2020	Swizzle	Swizzle	Highball glass	Lemon wheel

MR. SWIZZLE

This refreshing and tropical swizzle was the winner of the first-ever Coffee Cocktail Challenge hosted by myself in conjunction with Mr Black Spirits in 2020.

Nathan Robinson set out to create a beautiful and bright cocktail that showcased Mr Black Cold Brew Coffee Liqueur in a new light. Moving away from the heavy, night-time flavours commonly associated with coffee liqueurs, he incorporated light yet complex flavours to create a perfect daytime sipper.

The swizzle showcases Mr Black alongside a rich demerara rum and a spicy falernum and is rounded out with sweet notes of honey and refreshing citrus zest.

1½ oz (45ml) **demerara rum**
(Hamilton 86 recommended)

¾ oz (22.5ml) **coffee liqueur**
(Mr Black recommended)

½ oz (15ml) **falernum**

½ oz (15ml) **honey syrup**
(page 29)

½ oz (15ml) freshly squeezed
lemon juice

2 dashes of **orange bitters**
(1 dash Fee Brothers + 1 dash
Regans recommended)

1 In a highball glass, combine all ingredients.

2 Add pebble ice until ¾ full and swizzle until the glass frosts up.

3 Top with more pebble ice and garnish with a lemon wheel.

Practice your swizzling by making a **Queens Park Swizzle**
(page 231).

ORIGINATED	TYPE	METHOD	GLASSWARE	GARNISH
2005	Sour	Shaken	Coupe glass	None

NUCLEAR DAIQUIRI

The Nuclear Daiquiri was created by the late Gregor de Gruyther whilst at LAB (London Academy of Bartenders) bar in London in 2005. A classic **Daiquiri** (page 200) calls for a lighter-style Cuban rum whilst the Nuclear Daiquiri features a high-proof, full-flavoured Jamaican rum and herbal Green Chartreuse.

1 oz (30ml) **overproof rum** (Wray & Nephew recommended)

¾ oz (22.5ml) **Green Chartreuse**

¼ oz (7.5ml) **falernum**

1 oz (30ml) freshly squeezed **lime juice**

1 In a cocktail shaker, combine all ingredients.

2 Add ice and shake for 10 to 12 seconds.

3 Double strain into a chilled coupe glass.

A little overpowering? Try a lighter, lower-proof rum. (Although then you can't really call it nuclear!)

RUM

ORIGINATED	TYPE	METHOD	GLASSWARE	GARNISH
1970s	Tropical	Shaken	Old-fashioned glass	Grated nutmeg

PAINKILLER

The Painkiller was first created back in the 1970s by Daphne Henderson at the Soggy Dollar Bar on the Virgin Islands. There was no dock on the beach, so guests were forced to disembark directly into the shallows, leaving them with wet dollar bills (hence the name of the bar).

The founder of Pusser's rum, Charles Tobias, was friends with Daphne. He strived to acquire her recipe, but she kept it a trade secret. He eventually took one of her concoctions and replicated it before trademarking both the name and recipe, claiming them as his own. Pusser's then sued well-known New York bartenders who opened a bar named Painkiller, forcing them to change the bar to PKNY. The backlash from the bartending community was fierce.

1½ oz (45ml) **Demerara rum**

1½ oz (45ml) **pineapple juice**

½ oz (15ml) freshly squeezed **orange juice**

¾ oz (22.5ml) **cream of coconut** (page 30)

1 In a cocktail shaker, combine all ingredients.

2 Add ice and shake for 10 to 12 seconds.

3 Strain over pebble ice into an old-fashioned glass.

4 Garnish with grated nutmeg.

Avoid getting sued. Use Pusser's rum.

ORIGINATED	TYPE	METHOD	GLASSWARE	GARNISH
1954	Tropical	Blended	Hurricane glass	Pineapple wedge

PIÑA COLADA

The Piña Colada was created by Ramón Marrero in 1954 and was the welcome drink served to guests on arrival at the Caribe Hilton. Whilst it's commonly served as a blended frozen drink, I prefer a different approach by shaking or flash blending it with pebble ice. I also like a small amount of fresh lime juice for some acidity.

I recommend utilising slightly different recipes depending on your chosen method. If you prefer to blend your Piña Colada, use the following recipe, which is true to the original Caribe Hilton recipe: 2 ounces (60ml) lightly aged rum, 1 ounce (30ml) coconut cream, 1 ounce (30ml) heavy cream, 6 ounces (180ml) unsweetened pineapple juice, and ½ cup crushed ice.

The Piña Colada became so iconic that it was named the official drink of Puerto Rico in 1978.

2 oz (60ml) lightly aged **rum**

1½ oz (45ml) **pineapple juice**

1½ oz (45ml) **cream of coconut** (page 30)

½ oz (15ml) freshly squeezed **lime juice**

1 In a milkshake maker tin, combine all ingredients.

2 Add pebble ice and flash blend.

3 Transfer to a hurricane glass and top with more pebble ice, if needed.

4 Garnish with a pineapple wedge or spear.

If you don't have a milkshake maker, you can whip shake this drink (see page 38).

ORIGINATED	TYPE	METHOD	GLASSWARE	GARNISH
1694	Punch	Flash blended	Highball glass	Mint sprig

PLANTER'S PUNCH

Punch is the oldest family of mixed drinks (dating back to 1632) although it took 62 years for punch to make its way, along with the spice trade, to the Caribbean, where the Planter's Punch originated.

The traditional formula for Punch is: "one of sour, two of sweet, three of strong, four of weak—and a touch of spice to make it nice." The team from Smuggler's Cove followed this formula whilst creating their house Planter's Punch, which includes some of the most popular ingredients in Jamaica (Angostura bitters, allspice liqueur, and locally produced rum).

3 oz (90ml) aged **Jamaican rum**

¼ oz (7.5ml) **allspice dram**

1 oz (30ml) freshly squeezed **lime juice**

¾ oz (22.5ml) **demerara syrup** (page 28)

2 dashes of **Angostura bitters**

1 In a milkshake mixer tin, combine all ingredients.

2 Add pebble ice and flash blend.

3 Transfer the contents of the tin to a highball glass and top with more pebble ice, if needed.

4 Garnish with a mint sprig.

Try making your own house punch using the traditional formula.

If you don't have a milkshake maker, you can whip shake this drink (see page 38).

ORIGINATED
Circa 1930

TYPE
Tropical

METHOD
Flash blend

GLASSWARE
Footed pilsner

GARNISH
Lime wedge

PORT-AU-PRINCE

The Port-au-Prince is a creation of Don the Beachcomber from the 1930s and is named after the capital of Haiti.

One of Haiti's most well-known exports is Rhum Barbancourt. This highly regarded rum is made from raw cane juice instead of molasses, much like rhum agricole, although it doesn't fall into the category of French-style AOC (controlled designation of origin) certifications. Whilst it is made from raw cane juice, it's double-distilled to a higher proof, which makes it less grassy and lighter compared to a rhum agricole.

Given that the drink is named after the Haitian capital, it would be remiss not to use a Haitian rum.

1½ oz (45ml) aged **Haitian rum** (Rhum Barbancourt recommended)

½ oz (15ml) **falernum**

½ oz (15ml) **pineapple juice**

½ oz (15ml) freshly squeezed **lime juice**

¼ oz (7.5ml) **demerara syrup** (page 28)

1 dash of **grenadine** (page 30)

1 dash of **Angostura bitters**

1   In a milkshake maker tin, combine all ingredients.

2   Add pebble ice and flash blend.

3   Transfer to a footed pilsner glass and top with more pebble ice, if needed.

4   Garnish with a lime wedge.

Want a bit more rum? Try increasing and splitting the rum. For example: 1 ounce (30ml) Haitian rum and 1 ounce (30ml) demerara rum.

If you don't have a milkshake maker, you can whip shake this drink (see page 38).

ORIGINATED	TYPE	METHOD	GLASSWARE	GARNISH
1938	Tropical	Swizzle	Collins or highball glass	Mint sprig

QUEEN'S PARK SWIZZLE

The Queen's Park Swizzle evolved from the Green Swizzle, a drink that emerged from the Bridgetown Club in Barbados in the 1890s. The Green Swizzle was hugely popular in the Caribbean for 40 years following its creation and was adopted and refined by the Queen's Park Hotel in Trinidad. It led to a number of variations, including the Queen's Park Swizzle.

The drink evolves as it's consumed and has prominent notes of cinnamon and clove on the nose due to the layered Angostura bitters atop the drink.

4–6 **mint leaves**

½ oz (15ml) freshly squeezed **lime juice**

½ oz (15ml) **demerara syrup** (page 28)

2 oz (60ml) **demerara rum**

2–4 dashes of **Angostura bitters**

1 In a Collins or highball glass, gently muddle the mint leaves with the lime juice and demerara syrup.

2 Add the rum and fill the glass ¾ full with crushed ice. Swizzle until the glass frosts up.

3 Top with more crushed ice and finish with Angostura bitters.

4 Garnish with a mint sprig and serve with a straw.

Demerara rum is made in Guyana, but at the time the Queen's Park Swizzle was created, it was the most prevalent rum in Trinidad. You could also use a black rum, such as Coruba or Hamilton 86.

ORIGINATED	TYPE	METHOD	GLASSWARE	GARNISH
1947	Tropical	Shaken	Coupe glass	Lime wheel

ROYAL BERMUDA YACHT CLUB

The Royal Bermuda Yacht Club (venue) was established in Bermuda in 1844 and was frequented by British Army Officers. It was here that Trader Vic crafted this tiki-style version of a **Daiquiri** (page 200) featuring orange curaçao and spiced falernum to intensify the tropical flavours.

2 oz (60ml) aged **rum**

½ oz (15ml) **falernum**

¼ oz (7.5ml) **orange curaçao** (Pierre Ferrand recommended)

¾ oz (22.5ml) freshly squeezed **lime juice**

1   In a cocktail shaker, combine all ingredients.

2   Add ice and shake for 10 to 12 seconds.

3   Double strain into a chilled coupe glass.

4   Garnish with a lime wheel.

This cocktail works exceptionally well with a Caribbean orange liqueur in place of the curaçao. Try Clément Créole Shrubb, which is a maceration of Créole spices and bitter orange peels in a blend of rhum agricole.

ORIGINATED	TYPE	METHOD	GLASSWARE	GARNISH
1920s	Highball	Built	Highball glass	Lime wedge

RUM MULE

This drink is a slight variation on the Dark 'n' Stormy, which was created in the 1920s and has since been trademarked and fiercely protected by the Goslings family. The rum used for a Dark 'n' Stormy, Goslings Black Seal Rum, is a blend of distillates from Caribbean islands as the Goslings don't have a distillery of their own. The drink was originally mixed with Barritt's Ginger Beer.

A Dark 'n' Stormy made using an alternate rum is referred to as a Rum Mule or a Safe Harbour.

4 oz (120ml) **ginger beer**

1½ oz (45ml) **black rum**
(Coruba recommended)

1 Fill a highball glass with ice and add the ginger beer, stopping short from the top of the glass.

2 Float the rum on top.

3 Garnish with a lime wedge.

Stick with a black rum such as Coruba or Cruzan Blackstrap floated on top of the drink for a traditional Safe Harbour.

ORIGINATED	TYPE	METHOD	GLASSWARE	GARNISH
1940s	Tropical	Flash blended	Highball glass	Edible flowers

SCORPION

The Scorpion Bowl is another creation of Trader Vic and, as the name implies, is typically served in a punch bowl designed for communal consumption. This adjusted single-serve recipe is one of the more popular versions of the Scorpion by Steve Crane, the former owner of The Luau, a legendary Beverly Hills bar.

1 oz (30ml) gold **Puerto Rican rum**

1 oz (30ml) **gin**

½ oz (15ml) **brandy**

1 oz (30ml) freshly squeezed **orange juice**

½ oz (15ml) freshly squeezed **lime juice**

½ oz (15ml) **orgeat** (page 30)

⅓ oz (10ml) **simple syrup** (page 28)

1   In a milkshake maker tin, combine all ingredients.

2   Add pebble ice and flash blend.

3   Transfer to a highball glass and top with more pebble ice, if needed.

4   Garnish with edible flowers.

Entertaining? Multiply the ingredients and serve it in a punch bowl!

If you don't have a milkshake maker, you can whip shake this drink (see page 38).

ORIGINATED	TYPE	METHOD	GLASSWARE	GARNISH
Circa 1945	Tropical	Flash blended	Footed pilsner	Cherries, pineapple

THREE DOTS AND A DASH

Three Dots and a Dash is a tiki classic created during World War II by the godfather of tiki, Donn Beach (a.k.a. Don the Beachcomber). The name means "victory" in Morse code.

The recipe calls for a rhum agricole, which imparts a grassy, vegetal note to the drink. The cocktail also features typical tropical ingredients including aged rum, citrus, and spice. The allspice dram (also known as pimento dram) adds accents of cinnamon, clove, and nutmeg.

This particular recipe is from a Chicago tiki bar named after the cocktail, Three Dots and a Dash. Don's original recipe contained orange juice whilst the bar owner, Paul McGee, subs in dry curaçao.

1 oz (30ml) **rhum agricole**

1 oz (30ml) **demerara rum**

½ oz (15ml) **dry curaçao**

½ oz (15ml) **falernum**

¼ oz (7.5ml) **allspice dram**

1 oz (30ml) freshly squeezed **lime juice**

½ oz (15ml) **honey syrup** (page 29)

3 dashes of **Angostura bitters**

1   In a milkshake maker tin, combine all ingredients.

2   Add pebble ice and flash blend.

3   Transfer to a footed pilsner or highball glass and top with more pebble ice, if needed.

4   Garnish with 3 skewered cherries and a chunk of pineapple.

The garnish reflects the cocktail's name; cherries are the dots and the pineapple is the dash.

If you don't have a milkshake maker, you can whip shake this drink (see page 38).

ORIGINATED	TYPE	METHOD	GLASSWARE	GARNISH
1890	Tropical	Built	Old-fashioned glass	Lime

TI' PUNCH

The Ti' Punch is the national drink of the French Islands of Martinique. Distillers on the island save their very best rhum for their unaged spirit and the Ti' Punch is more commonly prepared with this blanc rhum. Undiluted and served at room temperature, the Ti' Punch is simple to prepare yet complex with flavour.

For the unfamiliar, the first sip may be daunting, but the aromatics are undeniable. Each sip will uncover notes of grassy, tropical fruit and fresh cane sugar.

The Ti' Punch is traditionally served unprepared with a full bottle of rhum agricole so you can prepare the drink yourself at the table.

2 oz (60ml) **rhum agricole**

1 tsp **cane syrup** (see note)

Small chunk of **lime**

1 To an old-fashioned glass, add the rum and cane syrup and stir to combine.

2 Squeeze 6 to 10 drops of lime juice into the drink and then add the spent lime to the glass.

Cane syrup can be purchased or made at home using the same method as simple syrup. (See page 28; replace white sugar with cane sugar.) Cane syrup has a slightly darker colour than simple syrup because the sugar isn't as refined. Simple syrup can be substituted if preferred.

ORIGINATED	TYPE	METHOD	GLASSWARE	GARNISH
Circa 1934	Tropical	Flash blended	Highball glass	Mint sprig

ZOMBIE

The Zombie joins the long list of Don the Beachcomber creations. It was one of the most popular drinks in the 1930s and was listed on the menu with a safety warning "only two to a customer" due to its generous pour of rums. (A wise drinker will adhere to this recommendation!)

Don's recipes were highly guarded. He would often create his own mixes to prevent others from copying his drinks. Not even his bartenders would know the exact recipe. The mystery ingredient in the Zombie, known as Don's Mix, was only recently discovered by Jeff "Beachbum" Berry in the notebook of the Beachcomber's head waiter, Dick Santiago.

1½ oz (45ml) gold **Puerto Rican rum**

1½ oz (45ml) aged **Jamaican rum**

1 oz (30ml) **overproof demerara rum**

¾ oz (22.5ml) freshly squeezed **lime juice**

½ oz (15ml) **Don's Mix** (see note)

½ oz (15ml) **falernum**

6 drops of **Pernod**

1 tsp **grenadine** (page 30)

1 dash of **Angostura bitters**

1 In a milkshake maker tin, combine all ingredients.

2 Add pebble ice and flash blend.

3 Transfer to a highball glass and top with more pebble ice, if needed.

4 Garnish with a mint sprig.

To make Don's Mix, combine 2 parts white grapefruit juice and 1 part cinnamon syrup.

For cinnamon syrup, prepare simple syrup as directed on page 28. In a saucepan, heat the syrup over medium-high heat and add 3 cinnamon sticks. When boiling, remove from heat and let steep for 3 to 4 hours before bottling.

ORIGINATED	TYPE	METHOD	GLASSWARE	GARNISH
2008	Sour	Shaken	Coupe glass	None

CONQUISTADOR

The Conquistador is yet another creation by Sam Ross, creator of the **Penicillin** (page 95), the **Paper Plane** (page 92), and the **Too Soon?** (page 176). At its heart, it is simply a split-base variant on a sour featuring an aged rum and blanco tequila. The combination of ingredients mellows the tequila whilst retaining its agave and subtle vegetal notes.

1 oz (30ml) aged **Dominican rum**

1 oz (30ml) **blanco tequila**

¾ oz (22.5ml) **simple syrup** (page 28)

½ oz (15ml) freshly squeezed **lemon juice**

½ oz (15ml) freshly squeezed **lime juice**

2 dashes of **orange bitters**

½ oz (15ml) **egg white**

1   In a cocktail shaker, combine all ingredients

2   Dry shake (without ice) for 8 to 10 seconds.

3   Add ice and wet shake (with ice) for 10 to 12 seconds.

4   Double strain into a chilled coupe glass.

Try creating your own split-base sour by using two of your favourite spirits. Check out pages 42–43 to learn simple techniques for creating your own unique cocktails.

ORIGINATED	TYPE	METHOD	GLASSWARE	GARNISH
2019	Sour	Shaken	Old-fashioned glass	Tajin

DEAD MAN'S HANDLE

The Dead Man's Handle is a mouth-watering creation from Tiffany Kirk of Miss Carousel in Houston, Texas. The recipe format resembles a Mexican-inspired **Bitter Mai Tai** (page 191) with a combination of tequila, aperitivo, fresh lime, and nutty orgeat. The drink is finished with a Mexican chilli, lime, and salt seasoning called Tajin, bringing a burst of acidity to the drink.

1½ oz (45ml) **blanco tequila**

¾ oz (22.5ml) **Aperol**

½ oz (15ml) freshly squeezed **lime juice**

½ oz (15ml) **orgeat** (page 30)

1   In a cocktail shaker, combine all ingredients.

2   Add ice and shake for 10 to 12 seconds.

3   Strain over crushed ice into an old-fashioned glass.

4   Top with more crushed ice and garnish with a sprinkle of Tajin.

Use homemade orgeat to make a delicious drink (page 30).

ORIGINATED	TYPE	METHOD	GLASSWARE	GARNISH
2010	Flip	Shaken	Stemmed cocktail glass	Grated nutmeg

DEATH FLIP

"You don't wanna meet this cocktail in a dark alley." These were the only words used to describe the Death Flip cocktail when it was first featured on the menu at Black Pearl in Melbourne, Australia, in 2010. The unlikely combination of ingredients may scare off the more timid drinkers, yet the flip seems to subdue the wild trio into a rich, creamy, and herbaceous combination.

1 oz (30ml) **blanco tequila**

½ oz (15ml) **Yellow Chartreuse**

½ oz (15ml) **Jagermeister**

¼ oz (7.5ml) **simple syrup** (page 28)

1 whole **egg**

1. In a cocktail shaker, combine all ingredients.

2. Add ice and shake for 10 to 12 seconds.

3. Strain into a chilled, stemmed cocktail glass.

4. Garnish with grated nutmeg.

Always ensure you use fresh eggs with no cracks or blemishes. To test if an egg is fresh, place it in water and it will sink to the bottom.

ORIGINATED	TYPE	METHOD	GLASSWARE	GARNISH
1930s	Daisy	Shaken	Old-fashioned glass	Lime wedge

MARGARITA

As with so many classic cocktails, the origin of the Margarita is fiercely debated.

Margarita is the Spanish word for daisy, so it is likely that the Margarita evolved from the Daisy family of cocktails. The original Daisy of the 1870s consisted of spirit, citrus, orange cordial, gum syrup, and seltzer served over ice. A Tequila Daisy, consisting of tequila, orange liqueur, lime juice, and soda water, was only a short stride away from a Margarita.

I recommend sticking with a blanco tequila, but the salt and glassware is down to your personal preference. If you're making drinks for guests, then perhaps only salt half the rim. I've always viewed the Margarita as a party drink, so serving it in an old-fashioned glass on the rocks makes the most sense to me.

Salt (optional), to rim glass

2 oz (60ml) **blanco tequila**

1 oz (30ml) **Cointreau**

¾ oz (22.5ml) freshly squeezed **lime juice**

1   Rim an old-fashioned glass with salt, if desired.

2   In a cocktail shaker, combine all ingredients.

3   Add ice and shake for 10 to 12 seconds

4   Strain over ice into the old-fashioned glass.

5   Garnish with a lime wedge.

If you love the Margarita, try a **Tommy's Margarita** *(page 259).*

The use of Grand Marnier for the orange liqueur results in a Cadillac Margarita.

ORIGINATED	TYPE	METHOD	GLASSWARE	GARNISH
2011	Sour	Shaken	Coupe glass	None

NAKED + FAMOUS

Joaquin Simo, a partner at Pouring Ribbons in New York City, describes the Naked & Famous as "the bastard child born out of an illicit Oaxacan love affair between the classic Last Word and the Paper Plane." He created the tasty combination during his time at the iconic bar Death & Co in New York and recommends using the smokiest mezcal you can get your hands on.

¾ oz (22.5ml) **mezcal**

¾ oz (22.5ml) **Yellow Chartreuse**

¾ oz (22.5ml) **Aperol**

¾ oz (22.5ml) freshly squeezed **lime juice**

1 In a cocktail shaker, combine all ingredients. Add ice and shake for 10 to 12 seconds.

2 Double strain into a chilled coupe glass.

*Compare the Naked & Famous alongside the **Last Word** (page 152) and the **Paper Plane** (page 92).*

ORIGINATED	TYPE	METHOD	GLASSWARE	GARNISH
2007	Cocktail	Stirred	Old-fashioned glass	Flamed orange zest

OAXACA OLD FASHIONED

Phil Ward added the Oaxaca Old Fashioned to Death & Co's first menu in 2007. Mezcal was a relatively new addition to the cocktail scene at the time, and it was this drink, according to the Death & Co. team, that inspired countless other drinks with mezcal in a supporting role.

1½ oz (45ml) **reposado tequila**

½ oz (15ml) **mezcal**

1 tsp **agave nectar**

2 dashes of **Angostura bitters**

1   In a mixing glass, combine all ingredients.

2   Add ice and stir for 15 to 30 seconds.

3   Strain over a large ice cube into an old-fashioned glass.

4   Garnish with a flamed orange zest.

Xocolatl mole or chocolate bitters are excellent choices for alternative bitters.

ORIGINATED	TYPE	METHOD	GLASSWARE	GARNISH
1977	Highball	Built	Highball glass	Grapefruit wedge

PALOMA

The first combination of Squirt (grapefruit soda) and tequila was mentioned in the 1970s, but it wasn't referred to as the Paloma for another several decades. It's a simple highball with few ingredients but it started getting the "craft bar treatment" when it became more prominent in the United States around 2005.

It's worth comparing various grapefruit sodas, both store bought and fresh, and experimenting with incorporating spice into the salt rim. Personally, I like to add a pinch of salt to the drink itself rather than on the rim.

Salt (optional), to rim the glass

2 oz (60ml) **blanco tequila**

½ oz (15ml) freshly squeezed **lime juice**

3 oz (90ml) **grapefruit soda**

1 Rim a highball glass with salt, if desired.

2 Fill the glass with ice and add all ingredients. Stir gently to combine.

3 Garnish with a grapefruit wedge (or lime).

Try making your own grapefruit soda with fresh grapefruit juice, agave syrup, a pinch of salt, and soda water.

Popular grapefruit soda choices are the Mexican-made version of Squirt or Jarritos.

ORIGINATED	TYPE	METHOD	GLASSWARE	GARNISH
1987	Sour	Shaken	Old-fashioned glass	None

TOMMY'S MARGARITA

The Tommy's Margarita originates from Tommy's Mexican Restaurant in San Francisco and was first created in 1987. Julio Bermejo was the restaurant's second-generation owner. He swapped the triple sec of a traditional margarita for agave syrup to further highlight the tequila.

2 oz (60ml) **reposado tequila**

1 oz (30ml) freshly squeezed **lime juice**

1 oz (30ml) **agave syrup**

1   In a cocktail shaker, combine all ingredients.

2   Add ice and shake for 10 to 12 seconds.

3   Strain over ice into an old-fashioned glass.

Agave syrup is diluted agave nectar.

ORIGINATED
Circa 1915

TYPE
Miscellaneous

METHOD
Shaken

GLASSWARE
Stemmed
cocktail glass

GARNISH
Grated nutmeg

BRANDY ALEXANDER

The original Alexander cocktail was first created around 1915, although the Brandy Alexander is far more well-known than its predecessor. Many would be surprised to discover that the original base spirit in the Alexander was gin and not brandy.

The Racquet Club's head bartender made the original Alexander to be served during the 1915 World Series in honour of Philadelphia's pitcher Grover Cleveland Alexander.

Two decades after its creation, written references started calling for brandy in place of gin and it then took over as the spirit of choice.

1 oz (30ml) **brandy**

1 oz (30ml) **brown crème de cacao**

1 oz (30ml) **heavy cream**

1   In a cocktail shaker, combine all ingredients.

2   Add ice and shake for 10 to 12 seconds.

3   Strain into a chilled stemmed cocktail glass.

4   Garnish with grated nutmeg.

Try comparing the two popular spirit options side by side—gin versus brandy.

You can easily create your own crème de cacao by macerating cacao nibs in high-proof vodka, filtering, and sweetening with cane sugar.

ORIGINATED	TYPE	METHOD	GLASSWARE	GARNISH
1853	Daisy	Shaken	Stemmed cocktail glass	Sugar rim, lemon peel

BRANDY CRUSTA

The Brandy Crusta was created by Joseph Santini, an Italian bartender in New Orleans, during the 1850s. Surprisingly, the drink predates the **Sazerac** (page 107), which is synonymous with New Orleans. During the late 1800s, a phylloxera outbreak decimated the French wine industry, and this event, followed by Prohibition, made it nearly impossible to acquire a bottle of cognac for several decades. As a result, the Brandy Crusta fell into obscurity until the early 2000s, when it was revived in New Orleans.

The original recipe calls for only small measurements of both lemon juice and gum syrup (sugar syrup with the addition of gum arabic to add viscosity), resulting in an unbalanced drink. This is a modern, adapted recipe, which has more lemon juice and uses maraschino liqueur in place of the original gum syrup.

Sugar, to rim the glass

1¾ oz (52.5ml) **cognac**

½ oz (15ml) **orange curaçao**

¼ oz (7.5ml) **maraschino liqueur** (Luxardo recommended)

¾ oz (22.5ml) freshly squeezed **lemon juice**

2 dashes of **Angostura bitters**

1 Rim a stemmed cocktail glass with sugar (see note).

2 In a cocktail shaker, combine all ingredients.

3 Add ice and shake for 10 to 12 seconds.

4 Double strain into the prepared glass.

5 Garnish with a large peel of lemon.

To rim your cocktail glass, simply run a spent lemon wedge around the rim of the glass to moisten before rolling the glass into the sugar to coat. Gently tap the glass to remove any excess sugar.

ORIGINATED	TYPE	METHOD	GLASSWARE	GARNISH
1920s	Sour	Shaken	Coupe glass	Lemon twist

CHAMPS-ÉLYSÉES

The Champs-Élysées is a careful balance of rich cognac and herbaceous Chartreuse with a pop of citrus that can produce a double take in even the most experienced of cocktail aficionados. The drink takes its name from the iconic strip in Paris that plays host to many of the city's cultural and social events and its landmark, the Arc de Triomphe.

The original recipe cited in the 1925 book *Drinks—Long & Short* by Nina Toye and Arthur H. Adair called for three glasses of brandy, one glass of Chartreuse, and one and a half glasses of sweetened lemon juice with a dash of Angostura bitters.

2 oz (60ml) **cognac**

½ oz (15ml) **Green Chartreuse**

¾ oz (22.5ml) freshly squeezed **lemon juice**

¼ oz (7.5ml) **simple syrup** (page 28)

2 dashes of **Angostura bitters**

1   In a cocktail shaker, combine all ingredients.

2   Add ice and shake for 10 to 12 seconds.

3   Double strain into a chilled coupe glass.

4   Garnish with a lemon twist.

Not a fan of Chartreuse? Try the **Sidecar** *(page 275), which features similar ingredients.*

ORIGINATED	TYPE	METHOD	GLASSWARE	GARNISH
1862	Flip	Blended	Old-fashioned glass	Grated nutmeg

EGGNOG

Jeffrey Morgenthaler spent years testing and refining his eggnog recipe. It's a classic eggnog similar to the recipe featured in Jerry Thomas' 1862 book *The Bartenders Guide*, which calls for both brandy and spiced rum. The key difference is the technique used to make the nog. Jerry Thomas' single-serve eggnog calls for shaking the drink, which adds dilution, whilst Jeffrey's batched recipe is made using a mixer and refrigerated, resulting in a rich, creamy, and flavourful eggnog.

2 large **eggs**

75 g superfine (caster) **sugar**

6 oz (180ml) **whole milk**

4 oz (120ml) **heavy cream**

2 oz (60ml) **brandy**

2 oz (60ml) **spiced rum** (Sailor Jerry's recommended)

1   In the bowl of a stand mixer with a whisk attachment, beat the eggs on medium speed for 1 minute.

2   Slowly add the sugar and blend for 1 minute more.

3   Add the milk, cream, brandy, and rum. Blend to incorporate.

4   Transfer to a sterilised glass bottle or jar and refrigerate overnight.

5   To serve, pour into a chilled old-fashioned glass and garnish with freshly grated nutmeg.

Compare this recipe with Jeffrey Morgethaler's tequila and sherry eggnog, which calls for 2 ounces (60ml) añejo tequila and 2½ ounces (75ml) amontillado sherry in place of the brandy and rum.

ORIGINATED	TYPE	METHOD	GLASSWARE	GARNISH
Circa 1974	Punch	Built	Punch bowl	Lemon wheels, grated nutmeg, edible flowers

FISH HOUSE PUNCH

The Fish House Punch originates from the oldest club in America, the Schuylkill Fishing Company in Pennsylvania. The recipe was passed from a club member, Charles G. Leland, to Jerry Thomas, who published it in his 1862 book. The original recipe calls for a peach brandy, although peach liqueur can be used in its place if peach brandy is unavailable.

There are a number of single-serve Fish House Punch recipes, but it is worth the time to prepare a large punch for sharing. Don't skip on the process for this punch—ensure you use the oleo-saccharum, tea is preferred over water, and a large, clear block of ice is best.

1 batch **oleo-saccharum** (page 31)

4 cups (1L) **Earl Grey tea** (or water)

4 cups (1L) **Jamaican rum**

2 cups (500ml) **cognac**

½ cup (125ml) **peach brandy**

1 cup (250ml) freshly squeezed **lemon juice**

1   In a large punch bowl, dissolve the oleo into the tea (or water).

2   Add the remaining ingredients and stir to mix.

3   Add a large, clear block of ice to the bowl.

4   Garnish with lemon wheels, freshly grated nutmeg, and edible flowers.

Use directional freezing in a cooler to create a big, clear ice block (see page 32). Freeze lemon wheels and flowers in the ice for effect.

ORIGINATED	TYPE	METHOD	GLASSWARE	GARNISH
Circa 1862	Miscellaneous	Shaken	Old-fashioned glass	Grated nutmeg

MILK PUNCH

Milk Punch was featured in Jerry Thomas' *The Bartenders Guide* in 1862. It's a simple, four-ingredient cocktail that is quick to prepare and best suited for serving after dinner as a dessert drink.

This version should not be confused with the fashionable Clarified Milk Punch (also known as English Milk Punch), which dates to the seventeenth century and takes far longer to prepare. Clarified Milk Punch combines spirit, sugar, lemon, and milk, which curdles. Filtering the mixture removes the curds and leaves the milk whey, resulting in a smooth and silky, transparent drink.

1 oz (30ml) **cognac**

1 oz (30ml) **aged rum**

1½ oz (45ml) **whole milk**

¾ oz (22.5ml) **simple syrup** (page 28)

1 In a cocktail shaker, combine all ingredients.

2 Add ice and shake for 10 to 12 seconds.

3 Strain over a large ice cube into an old-fashioned glass.

4 Garnish with freshly grated nutmeg.

Try adding vanilla extract or use maple syrup as the sweetener.

Eggnog *(page 267) is a variation of milk punch, also known as Egg Milk Punch.*

ORIGINATED	TYPE	METHOD	GLASSWARE	GARNISH
1903	Sour	Shaken	Old-fashioned glass	Aromatic bitters

PISCO SOUR

Victor Morris, proprietor of an American bar in Lima, Peru, was long credited for the creation of the Pisco Sour—that is until a Peruvian journalist discovered that a similar recipe had been published in a Peruvian cooking manual in 1903, 13 years prior to Victor opening his bar.

Whilst the history of the drink is a little hazy, it has become incredibly popular in Peru and neighbouring Chile, with both countries claiming it as their national drink.

2 oz (60ml) **pisco**

¾ oz (22.5ml) freshly squeezed **lime juice**

¾ oz (22.5ml) **simple syrup** (page 28)

½ oz (15ml) **egg white**

5–6 drops of **Amargo Chuncho bitters** (or Angostura bitters)

1   In a cocktail shaker, combine all ingredients except the bitters.

2   Dry shake (without ice) for 8 to 10 seconds.

3   Add ice and shake for 10 to 12 seconds.

4   Double strain into a chilled old-fashioned glass (or a stemmed cocktail glass).

5   Finish with drops of bitters.

International Pisco Sour Day is celebrated around the world on the first Saturday in February every year.

ORIGINATED	TYPE	METHOD	GLASSWARE	GARNISH
Circa 1919	Daisy	Shaken	Coupe glass	Orange twist

SIDECAR

The first mention of the Sidecar was in Harry McElhone's *ABC of Mixing Drinks* in 1919. Harry credits the drink's invention to Pat MacGarry, a bartender at the Buck's Club in London at the time. The recipe was an equal part affair, which differs to how most bartenders serve it today. The earliest versions lacked a sugar rim but applying the sugared rim became common practice from the 1930s.

2 oz (60ml) **cognac** (Pierre Ferrand 1840 recommended)

¾ oz (22.5ml) **dry curaçao** (Pierre Ferrand recommended)

¾ oz (22.5ml) freshly squeezed **lemon juice**

1 tsp **demerara syrup** (page 28)

1 In a cocktail shaker, combine all ingredients.

2 Add ice and shake for 10 to 12 seconds.

3 Double strain into a chilled coupe glass.

4 Garnish with an orange twist.

You can replace the dry curaçao with an alternate orange liqueur, such as Cointreau, although you may need to omit the demerara syrup to keep it balanced.

ORIGINATED	TYPE	METHOD	GLASSWARE	GARNISH
Circa 1937	Vermouth cocktail	Stirred	Old-fashioned glass	Lemon twist

VIEUX CARRÉ

The creation of the Vieux Carré is attributed to Walter Bergeron, head bartender at the Hotel Monteleone in New Orleans' French Quarter during the 1930s. It was first published in Stanley Arthur's *Famous New Orleans Drinks and How to Mix Them* in 1937. The drink can still be enjoyed at the Hotel Monteleone's Carousel Bar & Lounge.

1 oz (30ml) **cognac**

1 oz (30ml) **rye whiskey**

1 oz (30ml) **sweet vermouth**

¼ oz (7.5ml) **Benedictine**

2 dashes of **Angostura bitters**

2 dashes of **Peychaud's bitters**

1   To a mixing glass, add all ingredients.

2   Add ice and stir for 15 to 30 seconds.

3   Strain over a large ice cube into an old-fashioned glass.

4   Garnish with a twist of lemon.

The Vieux Carré is best made with a higher proof whiskey such as Rittenhouse 100-proof rye.

ORIGINATED	TYPE	METHOD	GLASSWARE	GARNISH
Circa 1924	Highball	Built	Collins glass	Celery, lemon wedge

BLOODY MARY

The drink was first created by Fernand "Pete" Petiot at Harry's New York Bar in Paris around 1924. A decade or so later, after the abolishment of Prohibition, he was hired at the King Cole Room in New York City. Vodka was yet to become readily available in the United States, so he started serving his tomato juice concoction with gin. The hotel management disliked the name "Bloody Mary," as it was too vulgar, so it was renamed the Red Snapper.

The Bloody Mary is well known for being the ultimate hangover cure. Personally, I strongly dislike tomato juice in drinks so I stay well clear of this one, but it still plays an important role in a bartender's repertoire.

2 oz (60ml) **vodka**

4 oz (120ml) **tomato juice**

¼ oz (7.5ml) freshly squeezed **lemon juice**

4 dashes of **Tabasco sauce**

2 dashes of **Worcestershire sauce**

Pinch of **salt** and **pepper**

1 In a cocktail shaker, combine all ingredients.

2 Add ice and swirl the shaker to chill and combine the ingredients. (Alternatively, pour back and forth from one tin to another, a technique known as "throwing.")

3 Strain over fresh ice into a Collins glass and garnish with a stick of celery and a lemon wedge.

Use this as a base recipe and make it your own—try it with celery salt, horseradish, hot sauce, etc., or substitute the vodka for another spirit, such as mezcal.

Variations include the Bloody Maria (tequila), the Red Snapper (gin) and the Caesar (clamato juice).

ORIGINATED	TYPE	METHOD	GLASSWARE	GARNISH
1980s	Daisy	Shaken	Stemmed cocktail glass	Lemon peel

COSMOPOLITAN

The Cosmopolitan or "Cosmo" is an iconic 1980s cocktail that became synonymous with the television series *Sex and the City* in the late 1990s.

Toby Cecchini was working at The Odeon in Tribeca in 1988 when he set out to make a tasty riff on a pink cocktail a waitress had requested that was making its way around San Francisco—a mix of rail vodka, Rose's lime juice, and grenadine. Utilising the fresh ingredients on hand, he built his own version of the pink drink as a simple sour with Absolut Citron vodka, Cointreau, fresh lime juice, and Ocean Spray cranberry juice, serving it up with a lemon twist.

It seems as though the Cosmo—one of the few cocktails to emerge from the '80s—has a very reluctant creator in Cecchini, who refers to the drink as his "albatross" and who is still astounded by its resilience and continued popularity for over three decades.

2 oz (60ml) **Absolut Citron**

1 oz (30ml) **Cointreau**

1 oz (30ml) freshly squeezed **lime juice**

1 oz (30ml) **cranberry juice**

1   In a cocktail shaker, combine all ingredients.

2   Add ice and shake for 10 to 12 seconds.

3   Double strain into a chilled, stemmed cocktail glass.

4   Garnish with a lemon peel.

Not a vodka fan? There is another version of the Cosmopolitan that predates this recipe. The older version is now referred to as the 1934 Cosmopolitan and features a gin base with raspberry syrup.

ORIGINATED	TYPE	METHOD	GLASSWARE	GARNISH
2010	Sour	Shaken	Old-fashioned glass	Passionfruit, mint sprig

EAST 8 HOLD UP

The East 8 Hold Up was created by Kevin Armstrong, a bartender at London's Milk & Honey, in 2010. Kevin and a friend were returning home one evening through the E8 area of London, when his friend was mugged with his pants down. They nicknamed the mugging the East 8 Hold Up, which later gave inspiration to the drink.

1½ oz (45ml) **vodka**

½ oz (15ml) **Aperol**

¾ oz (22.5ml) **pineapple juice**

½ oz (15ml) freshly squeezed **lime juice**

½ oz (15ml) **simple syrup** (page 28)

1 tsp (5ml) **passion fruit syrup**

1 In a cocktail shaker, combine all ingredients.

2 Add ice and shake for 10 to 12 seconds.

3 Strain over fresh ice into an old-fashioned glass.

4 Garnish with half a passionfruit and a mint sprig.

ORIGINATED	TYPE	METHOD	GLASSWARE	GARNISH
1980s	Miscellaneous	Shaken	Coupe glass	Coffee beans

ESPRESSO MARTINI

Dick Bradsell first created the Espresso Martini in the 1980s. Legend has it that he made the drink for a supermodel when she requested something that would "wake me up and f*ck me up." He combined Wyborowa, a Polish rye-grain vodka, and Kahlúa, a rum-based coffee liqueur, with fresh espresso and a touch of simple syrup for sweetness.

Australia's obsession with coffee has resulted in the Espresso Martini becoming a crowd favourite in bars, where it outsells all other cocktails.

2 oz (60ml) **vodka**
½ oz (15ml) **coffee liqueur**
1 oz (30ml) fresh **espresso**
¼ oz (7.5ml) **simple syrup**
    (page 28)

1   In a cocktail shaker, combine all ingredients.

2   Add ice and shake vigorously for 10 to 12 seconds.

3   Double strain into a chilled coupe glass.

4   Garnish with 3 coffee beans.

Use fresh espresso and give a strong shake to ensure a thick crema.

Cold drip coffee is a great alternative to freshly brewed coffee, especially when entertaining and larger numbers of cocktails are required.

ORIGINATED	TYPE	METHOD	GLASSWARE	GARNISH
1970s	Sour	Shaken	Martini glass	Sugar rim

LEMON DROP

The Lemon Drop was introduced in the 1970s by Norman Jay Hobday, a returning Vietnam veteran who decided to try his hand at bartending by opening the area's first fern bar filled with foliage and drinks. The drink dominated cocktail menus for several decades to follow.

The drink's signature sugar rim adds a sweet introduction to the sour cocktail. It is also commonly served as a shooter.

Sugar, to rim glass

2 oz (60ml) **vodka**

¼ oz (7.5ml) **Cointreau**

¾ oz (22.5ml) freshly squeezed **lemon juice**

¾ oz (22.5ml) **simple syrup** (page 28)

1 Rim a chilled martini glass with sugar (see note).

2 In a cocktail shaker, combine all ingredients.

3 Add ice and shake for 10 to 12 seconds.

4 Double strain into the prepared glass.

To rim your cocktail glass, simply run a spent lemon wedge around the rim of the glass to moisten before rolling the glass into the sugar to coat. Gently tap the glass to remove any excess sugar.

ORIGINATED	TYPE	METHOD	GLASSWARE	GARNISH
1940s	Highball	Built	Copper mug	Lime wedges

MOSCOW MULE

The Moscow Mule was one of the key cocktails that spearheaded the rise in popularity of vodka in the United States. Smirnoff vodka was new in the States at a time when most people were drinking beer and whiskey, so John Martin, the U.S. Smirnoff distributor, had a hard task ahead.

John met with bar owner and ginger beer producer Jack Morgan for an alcohol-fueled marketing meeting. Around the same time, John's girlfriend, Ozaline Schmidt, had inherited a copper factory and the company's mugs weren't moving. With a stroke of marketing genius, they made the simplest of concoctions, served it in a copper mug, and named it the Moscow Mule.

2 oz (60ml) **vodka**

½ oz (15ml) freshly squeezed **lime juice**

4 oz (120ml) **ginger beer**

1 To a copper mug, add the vodka and lime juice.

2 Fill the mug with ice and top with the ginger beer. Give a gentle stir to combine.

3 Garnish with a lime wedge.

Pick a good quality, spicy ginger beer—not ginger ale.

ORIGINATED	TYPE	METHOD	GLASSWARE	GARNISH
1838	Cobbler	Shaken	Highball glass	Seasonal fruit, mint, berries

SHERRY COBBLER

The Sherry Cobbler is one of the most underrated mixed drinks, especially considering that it was the most popular drink throughout much of the world during the mid- to late nineteenth century. It was apparently named for the cobbles of ice that are crucial to the construction of a cobbler.

Amontillado sherry is recommended, although it can be substituted with an alternate dry sherry. I like adding a touch of lemon to my cobblers; either ¼ ounce (7.5ml) freshly squeezed lemon juice, or a bit of lemon zest added to the ingredients prior to shaking.

4 oz (120ml) **Amontillado sherry**

½ oz (15ml) **simple syrup** (page 28)

2–3 **orange slices**

1 In a cocktail shaker, combine all ingredients.

2 Add about ½ cup pebble or crushed ice and shake to combine.

3 Transfer the contents of the shaker to a highball glass and top with more pebble or crushed ice.

4 Garnish with a mint sprig, seasonal fruit, and berries.

You may need to adjust the amount of simple syrup depending on your choice of sherry.

Citrus, pineapple, raspberries, strawberries, and mint are all ideal garnishing options.

ORIGINATED	TYPE	METHOD	GLASSWARE	GARNISH
1874	Flip	Shaken	Stemmed cocktail glass	Grated nutmeg

SHERRY FLIP

Flips have been around for well over three centuries and were commonly served as hot drinks consisting of beer, rum, and sugar. The drink evolved and was first referenced as a cold drink in 1874. The written reference in *The American Bar-Tender or the Art and Mystery of Mixing Drinks* by E. A. Simmons closely resembles this recipe: a mixture of spirit or fortified wine, sugar, and egg.

The Sherry Flip works exceptionally well with a rich, dry, and nutty Oloroso sherry.

2 oz (60ml) **Oloroso sherry**

½ oz (15ml) **simple syrup** (page 28)

1 whole **egg**

1   In a cocktail shaker, combine all ingredients.

2   Add ice and shake for 10 to 12 seconds.

3   Strain into chilled stemmed cocktail glass—a vintage glass is a nice touch—and garnish with grated nutmeg.

Did you enjoy the Sherry Flip? Try a Port Wine Flip (use a tawny) or Brandy Flip.

ORIGINATED	TYPE	METHOD	GLASSWARE	GARNISH
2003	Tropical	Swizzle	Highball or Collins glass	Mint sprig

CHARTREUSE SWIZZLE

The Chartreuse Swizzle was created by Marcovaldo Dionyso in San Francisco in 2003. He was a self-proclaimed Chartreuse fanatic and entered the local Chartreuse cocktail competition five years running. It was his fifth entry that captured the judges' attention.

Swizzles were not overly popular at the time, and the addition of falernum made it a completely left-of-field entry. The delicious tiki-fied, herbaceous swizzle stole the show and took the win.

It wasn't until 2010 when Marcovaldo started working at Smugglers Cove in San Francisco that the cocktail gained the popularity it deserved.

1½ oz (45ml) **Green Chartreuse**

½ oz (15ml) **Velvet falernum**

1 oz (30ml) **pineapple juice**

¾ oz (22.5ml) freshly squeezed **lime juice**

1 In a highball or Collins glass, combine all ingredients.

2 Add pebble ice to fill the glass three-quarters full. Swizzle until the glass frosts up.

3 Top with more pebble ice and garnish with a mint sprig. (Alternatively, garnish with pineapple spears and a lime wheel.)

Looking for a more subtle Green Chartreuse cocktail? Try the **Champs-Élysées** *(page 264).*

ORIGINATED	TYPE	METHOD	GLASSWARE	GARNISH
2010	Tropical	Flash blend	Highball glass	Mint sprig

PIÑA VERDE

This simple yet flavourful four-ingredient cocktail was created by Erick Castro whilst tending bar at Polite Provisions in San Diego. Erick's goal was to create a rich, herbaceous cocktail which, over several years of tweaking, resulted in this herbal variation on the classic Piña Colada. The name means "green pineapple" in Spanish, and sweet pineapple and coconut tame the usually dominant Green Chartreuse, allowing the herbs, spices, and botanicals to be identified and appreciated.

1½ oz (45ml) **Green Chartreuse**

1½ oz (45ml) **pineapple juice**

¾ oz (22.5ml) **cream of coconut** (page 30)

½ oz (15ml) freshly squeezed **lime juice**

1   In a milkshake maker tin, combine all ingredients.

2   Add pebble ice and flash blend.

3   Transfer the contents of the tin to a highball glass.

4   Top with more pebble ice and garnish with a mint sprig.

If you don't have a milkshake maker, you can whip shake this drink (see page 38).

ACKNOWLEDGMENTS

First and foremost I want to thank my wife, Kat. She spent countless hours researching, helping with photo shoots, and caring for Noah, the newest addition to our family, whilst I researched and wrote. She was crucial to the completion of the book and I appreciate everything she does for our little family. Thank you for everything you do. I love you dearly.

A huge thank you to my editor, Ann, for stumbling across my YouTube channel and for her impeccable attention to detail. Thank you for helping me clarify my words on paper and for the huge list of updates and improvements you made for me.

A big shout-out goes to my regular YouTube viewers, supporters, and everyone who has ever watched, liked, and enjoyed the content that I share. This book is only possible because of your support over the many years.

Thank you to my business partners at Threefold Distilling, Luke and Aidan, for putting in more than their fair share of hours covering for me at the distillery so that I could dedicate time to the book.

Thank you to Meaghan: you are a truly skilled photographer and I love the way you captured my cocktails. Much appreciation to Matt and Scott (Alfred's Bar) and Simon (Paloma Bar and Pantry) for letting me use their venues and an extra special shout-out goes to Tim and Tonic for producing amazing video content for the book.

And finally, thank you to DK Publishing for entrusting me to write this book and to everyone on the U.S. team who has helped my cocktail guide come to fruition.

To my friends and family: your patience has not gone unnoticed whilst I've focused on my work. Love you all.

PHOTO CREDITS AND PUBLISHER'S ACKNOWLEDGMENTS

Photos © Meaghan Coles: Cover, 9, 49, 61, 69, 74, 77, 86, 89, 101, 113, 122, 129, 137, 142, 150, 158, 169, 181, 189, 193, 209, 210, 213, 218, 245, 253, 254, 265, 274, 277. Photos © Steven Roennfeldt: 53, 57, 105, 118, 125, 161, 170, 177, 178, 182, 190, 197, 202, 214, 245, 246, 249, 269, 281, 289. All other images © Dorling Kindersley Limited.

DK Publishing would like to thank the following individuals for their participation in the photo shoot: Kalliopi Nikou (bartender), Daniel Showalter (photographer), Lovoni Walker (stylist).

INDEX

Steven Roennfeldt, better known as Steve the Bartender, has been sharing easy-to-follow cocktail videos on YouTube since 2017. He has created a catalogue of over 600 videos and built a huge community of passionate cocktail enthusiasts. Steve is continually amazed and humbled by the far-reaching impact of his work. While flavour fuels his curiosity, the cocktail community stirs his passion and pushes him to continue creating his entertaining and educational content.

When he isn't shaking up a storm, reinventing a cocktail list, or crafting gin, you'll find Steve at home with his family. Steve's wife, Kat, has shared in the flavoursome journey since the beginning, being his harshest critic yet biggest supporter, while his adorable son Noah observes from the sidelines. Steve and his family live in Adelaide, Australia.

Scan to connect with Steve!